It's another Quality Book from CGP

This book is for anyone doing GCSE Schools History Project.

Whatever subject you're doing it's the same
old story — there are lots of facts and you've just got
to learn them. KS4 History is no different.

Happily this CGP book gives you all that important
information as clearly and concisely as possible.

It's also got some daft bits in to try and make the whole
experience at least vaguely entertaining for you.

What CGP is all about

Our sole aim here at CGP is to produce the highest quality
books — carefully written, immaculately presented and
dangerously close to being funny.

Then we work our socks off to get them out to you
— at the cheapest possible prices.

Contents

History of the American West

Medicine Through Time

Published by Coordination Group Publications
Typesetting and layout by The History Coordination Group
Illustrations by Erik Blakeley, Ashley Tyson and Lex Ward
Co-edited and additional text by Glenn Rogers

Written by Erik Blakeley

ISBN: 978 1 84146 301 8

Groovy website: www.cgpbooks.co.uk
Printed by Elanders Hindson Ltd, Newcastle upon Tyne.
Clipart sources: CorelDRAW® and VECTOR.

Know Your Stuff — It's a Start

Learning the facts is a fair challenge — but that's only half the job. A brain full of facts is no good unless you can turn them into winning answers. Here's how...

Mountains of facts — which to learn, which to use?

1) First of all make sure you know whether your syllabus tells you what subject area paper two will be set on. You will need to know this area in much more detail than the rest.

2) Exam questions look for plenty of detailed facts — but just make sure the ones you use are relevant to the question. You won't get marks if they're not. You must be selective.

3) You get marks for how well you recall, select, organise and deploy what you learn...

a) **RECALL** means remembering the facts accurately.

b) **SELECT** means picking out the relevant facts for your answer.

c) **ORGANISE** means putting the facts you've chosen into the best order for answering the question.

d) **DEPLOY** means actually doing it right — using the right facts in the right order to answer a question.

Dates — less fun in history than the cinema

2001
A Space
Odyssey

1) We've tried to give you as many of the relevant dates as possible. This means that, unless you have a photographic memory, you won't remember all of them.

2) You need to use them to get sequences of events right.

3) You need to remember dates for the paper two topic specified in the syllabus for your year.

4) Some dates are more important than others and need to be learnt whether or not they're covered in paper two.

The California Gold Rush of 1849 is an example. Make a list of the ones you think are vital and learn them. When you've learnt those, pick out the next most important ones, and so on.

Always think about Causes and Consequences

1) Cause means the reason or reasons (there are often more than one) something happened — e.g. the causes of the Indian Wars, or the cholera epidemics in the 1830s and 40s. Any time you have a fact in History, think about what caused it and why it happened. There are reasons why any event takes place and it's your job to work them out.

2) Consequence means what happened because of an action — it's the result of an event, e.g. a consequence of the introduction of antiseptics was a fall in the post-operative death rate.

3) These two ideas fit together — think of them like a row of dominoes. The first domino is the cause which starts the others falling, and the last one is knocked down as a consequence or effect of all the others falling over.

CAUSE EFFECT CONSEQUENCE

Development and Exam Technique

Here's some stuff on the <u>development</u> of medicine — and on <u>Exam technique</u>.

Change and Continuity

1) <u>Change</u> is when something happens to make things <u>different</u> — there can be <u>quick</u> changes (like the effect of Pasteur's Germ theory on people's views of the causes of disease); or there can be <u>slow</u> changes (like the increase in life expectancies in the 20th century due to improvements in living conditions).

2) <u>Continuity</u> is the <u>opposite</u> of change — it's when something stays the <u>same</u> (like much of America before the arrival of the Whites, or the importance of Galen's writings for 1400 years).

3) These ideas are opposites — think of <u>continuity</u> as a <u>flat line</u> going along until there is a sudden <u>change</u> — and the line becomes a <u>zigzag</u>:

The Four Key Areas of Answer Writing

1) Fit your answer to the mark scheme

The more marks a question's worth, the more pieces of information you'll need in your answer. Include <u>one idea per mark</u>. Don't write a huge answer containing only one idea — you'll probably get one mark.

1) introduction
2) content
3) conclusion

2) Planning for perfection

<u>Sort out</u> what you want to say before you start writing — think about how to answer the question, what the <u>key words</u> are, and if ideas of <u>cause and effect</u>, or <u>change and continuity</u> will be useful. Scribble a list of your main points and work out the best order.

3) Giving the right content

Don't just chuck in everything you know. You've got to be <u>relevant</u> and <u>accurate</u> — e.g. if you're writing about Lady Montagu and inoculation, don't spend half the answer talking about camels on the Silk Road.

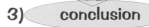

4) Clear writing Style

1) Use the <u>key words</u> from the question to explain what the essay is about.

2) <u>Explain</u> and <u>analyse</u> the question. Make sure each paragraph deals with a separate point in detail.

3) Use <u>facts</u> to support your ideas.

4) <u>Answer</u> the question by giving your opinion.

5) <u>Avoid</u> long, complicated sentences — make it easy for the <u>examiner</u> to see how much you know!

6) Remember that an extra <u>5%</u> is awarded for spelling, punctuation and grammar.

Give a full answer to the question — cover both sides of any argument.
Check your work before the end of the exam and correct it.

Themes and Factors

Always think how stuff you learn relates to these <u>themes</u> and <u>factors</u> — you'll be asked about them.

Themes

You have to be able to discuss the main themes below in each study — and trace their development across different periods. Look out for facts and events relevant to more than one theme. The arrows show the most obvious links for medicine.

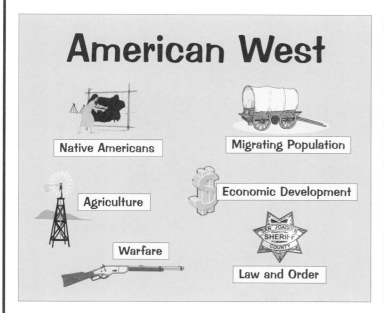

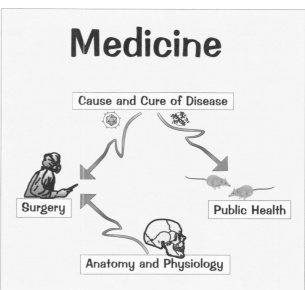

Factors

Certain factors occur again and again — influencing the development of our themes. Build up an answer on any development by thinking how each of these factors affected it.

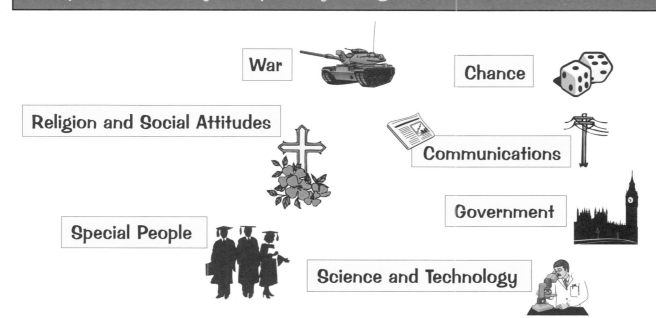

Geographical Regions

Right, the history of the American West. I suppose a pretty map would be a good place to start.

America has very different Geographical regions

When we speak of the American West, what we really mean is the area of North America west of the Mississippi River. This river runs from the northernmost region of present-day USA, right down to the Gulf of Mexico. In order to understand the events covered here, you need to examine how the environment has influenced the American people — so we'd better start with a look at the geography of North America. North America can be divided into several geographical regions, all of which are quite different from each other:

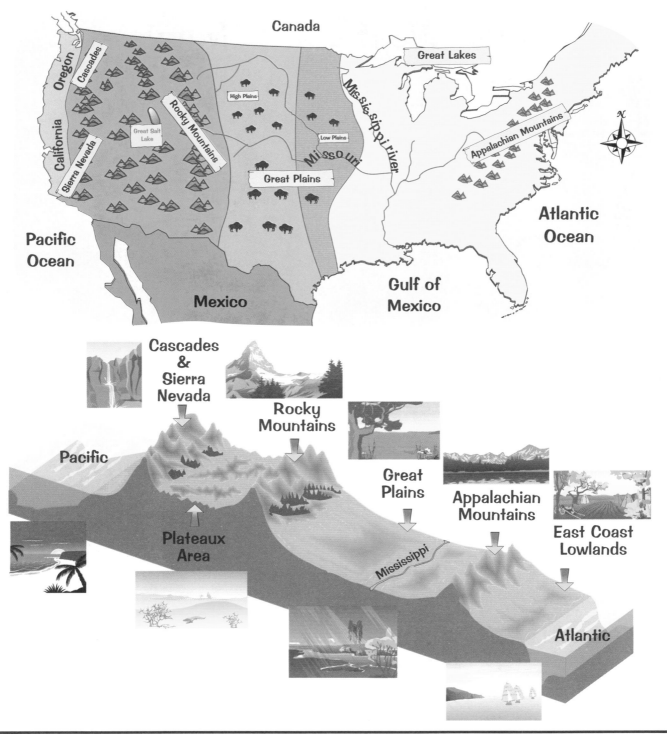

The West and its Climate

Enough of the maps. It's time to get down to the serious nitty-gritty.

The Great Plains lie in the centre of North America

1) Central North America is dominated by the Great Plains.
2) The Plains are mostly a huge, flat, expanse of grassland. There's two bits:
   — the "Low Plains" to the east, with long grass (remember L for Low and Long).
   — the "High Plains" to the west, with short grass.
3) The Great Plains become drier and more desert-like the further south you go.

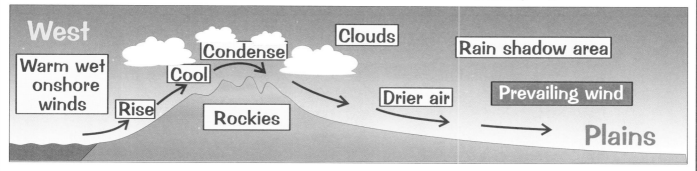

The Weather on the Plains is Extreme and scary

1) The weather across the Great Plains varies severely — it can make farming difficult even today.
2) The mountains on either side of the Plains produce rain shadows (regions with little rain). You often get droughts in the summer and severe snow in the winter.
3) Being so far from the sea means there's a huge difference in temperature between summer and winter.
4) Tornadoes are quite common — like the one that damaged Oklahoma City in 1999.
5) These extremes are described as a continental climate. By comparison Britain is never very far from the sea and has fairly even temperatures and mild weather — an example of a temperate climate.

The Rocky Mountains form a Barrier across America

1) The slopes on either side of the Rockies are heavily wooded –- especially in the South.
2) Towards the centre of the Rockies is the Plateaux region. This is relatively flat and contains areas of desert. Water can run onto the Plateaux region and get trapped, only escaping by evaporation. This has led to the Great Salt Lake — important later on.

The Pacific Coastlands are milder and fertile

1) West beyond the Sierra Nevada mountains lies the Pacific coastlands.
2) This land is mainly fertile. It has a pleasant climate because it is close to the sea.
3) This region was a much sought-after place to live. It still is, despite the earthquake risk.

You'd better learn the geography — or you're history...

OK, so you thought you were studying history. The thing is though, so much of what happened in the West was related to the geography. That means things'll make much more sense and be easier to remember if you learn some geography first. So without looking, try drawing the main features of the US, and label all the important bits. Then turn back and check — and repeat it if you've missed stuff. It's the only really sure way of learning something.

SECTION ONE — THE GEOGRAPHY OF AMERICA

Maps and Dates

Oh, another map. Here's where the main Indian <u>tribes</u> lived in <u>1840</u>, the start of the study period.

The Plains Indians had many different Tribes

<u>Native Americans</u> are commonly known as <u>Indians</u>. You can blame <u>Columbus</u> for that — he thought he'd reached <u>India</u> when he first got to America in <u>1492</u>. He soon realised he hadn't, but called the people Indians anyway. A slight lack of imagination there, I'd say.

Knowing the names of some of the tribes will make for more impressive answers — but only if you spell them right and put them in the right places.

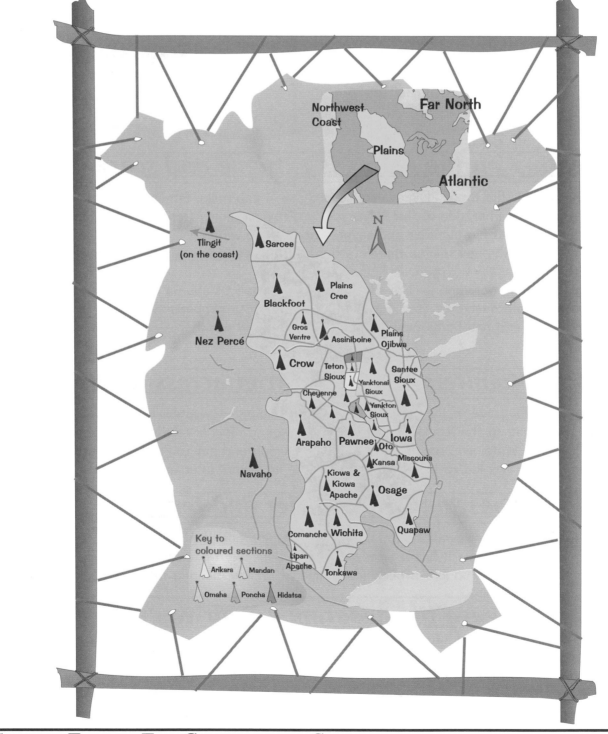

Lifestyles of the Native Americans

Understanding the different cultures is vital to understanding the problems between the Native Americans and the early White settlers.

The Natives were mostly Hunter-Gatherers

1) Most of the Plains Indians were nomadic hunters when the Whites first arrived. They relied very heavily on the buffalo — for food, clothing, tepees, bone tools and fuel (dried dung). They practised some agriculture, but much less after about 1800 — the arrival of horses had made hunting easier. Also European diseases such as smallpox and cholera had hit the farming populations very hard. Some tribes such as the Mandans were practically wiped out.

2) The Indians of the far west (California and Oregon) had a different culture — they relied heavily on craft and trade. The tribes in this area included the Tlingits. In the south the Navajos became successful shepherds after the introduction of sheep and goats.

3) Most Indians travelled from place to place to follow wild animals, so they didn't regard land as something that anyone owned. Even their agriculture was a very communal activity.

4) Most of the Whites who tried to settle permanently in the west were farmers or "homesteaders". They saw the vast empty spaces as a chance for land of their own.

5) Many of the homesteaders were poor people or those who had been treated with prejudice due to their race or religion — they had few chances in Europe or the Eastern USA.

Most Indian men were also Warriors

1) Native Americans mostly travelled in small bands of one or two extended families. Tribal gatherings would occur to make important decisions or in times of war.

2) Tribal warfare was part of the culture of many Indians. Men were expected to be hunters and warriors. Low intensity warfare helped unite tribes and raiding for animals and captives was part of life.

3) Symbolic acts of bravery reduced the need to kill or be killed — allowing warfare to be sustainable. War was never pretty though — death was always a risk.

4) This was very different from European culture at the time. In Europe armies were kept separate from the civilian population. Everyday life was supposed to be peaceful. Banditry and warfare for personal gain was regarded as despicable. During the American Civil War General Sherman had set out to crush the southern states by "Total War". The same attitudes were later carried into the Indian Wars.

More tribes and tribulations — if only life were simple...

Life would have been a lot simpler if there was only one tribe — for you and for the Indians. But you can't win them all. You don't of course need to know all the tribes, but learning a few would be really handy — so long as you spell them right. And you know how to check that. Don't you. And while you're learning that, a few facts about their way of life wouldn't go amiss.

Religion and Tradition of the Indians

The Native Americans had very different beliefs from the Whites.

The Great Spirit was at the centre of Indians' religion

"Wah'kon-tah is the sum of all things, the collective totality that always was—without beginning, without end. Neither a force nor a spirit, it is the inexplicable sharing-togetherness that makes all things, animate and inanimate, of equal value, equal importance, and equal consequence because they are all Wah'kon-tah simultaneously, their forms collectively creating the form of Wah'kon-tah which is, obviously, incapable of being anthropomorphised." — Sanders and Peek.

The above is a description of the Great Spirit by modern Native American scholars. Their beliefs can be summarised a little more clearly:

1) Humans are part of Nature and not masters over it.
2) The Great Spirit is not a sentient (conscious) entity in the way that the god of the Jewish, Christian and Muslim faiths is.
3) The Great Spirit cannot be given human characteristics (anthropomorphised). The Jewish, Christian and Muslim faiths see man as created in the image of god, and so see characteristics of god in man.
4) The meeting of science and spirituality in the modern Gaia concept of the world as one living organism has much in common with the Great Spirit.

Circles and animal spirits are important

1) Native American beliefs emphasise the interdependence of all things — they see all things as being connected. For this reason circles are spiritually important to them.
2) They believe that all things have spirits. Successful hunting relies on a sort of religious bargaining carried out through rituals including dances — as well as field craft and skill with the bow or rifle. Even non-living things like rocks and mountains have spirits. Activities like mining could easily be believed to upset the spirits.

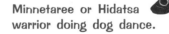

Minnetaree or Hidatsa
warrior doing dog dance.

Oral history means no books

1) Indians did not write history books. Important ideas and histories of their people were passed from generation to generation by telling stories.
2) Native American oral history has a tendency to make their history seem less changeable than it really was.
3) Oral history can also be fragile. The terrible epidemics already described killed off many of the old people, and many stories were lost with them.

Write it down — oral bet you won't remember it...

OK, more facts for you to learn — though not the Wah'kon-tah bit, of course. It can be useful to compare Indian beliefs with Christianity. Think of the similarities and differences, and think about why there was such a clash of cultures between the Indians and the Whites. Remember that even if you think you know it, you'll never know for sure until you try to write it down. So put pen to paper, and scribble down those facts. Do that and you'll know you know it.

Religion and Tradition of the Whites

Right, enough of the Indians' beliefs for now. It's time to look at what the Whites thought.

There's no getting away from the fact that the arrival of the White men and their culture was bad news for the Native Americans. Some terrible things were done.

The Whites Tried to Convert the Indians to Christianity

1) Christianity is a proselytising faith — it tries to convert people. Missionary work was seen as good, which meant other faiths and cultures were regarded as inferior.
2) Most of the Whites coming to America thought of the Indian religions as just savage superstition.

They also tried to impose their Culture on the Indians

1) The Whites had a great faith in their culture as well as in their religion. Most powerful Whites had an idealised picture of European society as the pinnacle of civilisation. They saw other cultures as failed attempts to achieve that ideal.
2) Teaching Indians to speak English and wear a shirt and tie was seen as a great kindness.
3) European culture had generated massive population and economic growth. These in turn led to the need for new space and resources.
Space and resources were what the American West was all about.

The Whites rarely stuck to their Treaties

1) The pace of change in America was too fast for both cultures.
2) American treaties with the Indians were almost always broken. This was partly because White men "spoke with forked tongue", but also because treaties made in good faith became nearly impossible to live up to following new discoveries. Examples include the discovery of gold in the Black Hills of Dakota, and the realisation that the Great Plains ("The Great American Desert") had the potential to be "America's Breadbasket".
3) In 1881 Helen Hunt Jackson wrote "A Century of Dishonour". It highlighted the unfair treatment of the Indians since the Whites started to move onto the Great Plains.

The Whites — more culture than a yeast yoghurt...

Not the prettiest picture of White culture, I'm afraid. You don't just need to learn the facts here — you need to think about them too. Exams rarely ask for specific facts. They'll ask for your opinions on things. Knowing lots of facts will of course help you to illustrate your opinions — but the facts by themselves won't get you very far. So whenever you learn stuff, think how it fits in with what you know already, and think what you think of it.

Manifest Destiny and Women's Roles

But that's not all. Many Whites believed they knew their future destiny too.

Many Christian Whites Believed in "Manifest Destiny"

1) Many White Americans believed that they were destined to occupy and govern all of North America. They saw it as their God-given right. They thought it was their "manifest destiny" to do so.

2) The term "manifest destiny" was actually coined by John L. O'Sullivan in 1845 over American relations with Mexico. The idea was used to justify wrongdoing in people's treatment of the Native Americans — they could blame God or fate rather than feeling guilt for their actions.

Women had very mixed fortunes in the American West

1) At first sight both the Indian and White settler cultures seem very macho and male-dominated. However in small Indian bands and families of homesteaders cooperation and hard work by all was needed for survival.

2) Women in Indian tribes made most of the finished goods. They owned the things they made, which gave them power and meant it was a brave man who made use of his ability to divorce his wife.

3) White women settlers worked side by side with men in the struggle to get farms off the ground — so they took part in much more decision-making than women in Europe or the East of America.

4) They were also largely responsible for housework and the education of their children.

5) Life for a homestead family varied between squalid catastrophe and near starvation to something approaching the ideal of "Little House on the Prairie".

Divine destiny — or a road to nowhere...

The role of women quite often comes up in Exam questions, so ignore this stuff at your peril. And Manifest Destiny is a pretty important concept to learn. But remember that such arrogant belief was far from universal — there were plenty of Whites who didn't believe in Manifest Destiny.

SECTION TWO — THE CLASH OF THE CULTURES

Revision Summary for Sections 1-2

Right, that's it for the geography and culture clash stuff. But before you plough straight into the next section, it's time for some questions. I know, I know, questions are boring. Yeah, it's all too easy to ignore stuff like this. It's all so interesting that you've just got to read the rest of the book straight away... The trouble is you'll soon forget it all if you don't go back over it. And if you forget it, you'll just have to relearn it later — frustrating and a bit of a hassle. Also, the more you learn now, the easier things'll be to learn later, because you'll be able to link new facts to the stuff you already know. So believe me, you really do want to work through these questions...

1) Why is the weather on the Great Plains so much more severe than that of Britain or the American coast?
2) What natural event seen on the Great Plains devastated Oklahoma City in 1999?
3) How was the Great Salt Lake formed?
4) Describe the vegetation on the Plains.
5) What feature of the Plains forced settlers to live in "sod houses"?
6) Which river approximately divides the "East" from the "West"?
7) Which river divides the Plains into a northern half and a southern half?
8) Why did Oregon and California attract the early migrants from the East?
9) What animal was at the centre of the nomadic hunter-gatherer lifestyle of the Plains Indians?
10) What two imports from Europe reduced the amount of agriculture practised by the Indians (one positive, one negative)?
11) Name and describe two tribes that didn't fit the hunter-gatherer stereotype.
12) "Cultural differences made conflict between the Whites and Native Americans inevitable." Discuss this statement.
13) Explain (in as much detail as you can) why the Europeans and the Indians saw the land of the West very differently.
14) Why is so little known of the history of America before the Whites arrived?
15) Many beliefs place great importance in circles. Discuss why this might be.
16) What is our place in the natural world according to: a) The Native Americans? b) The major faiths of Britain?
17) Are spiritual beliefs of the type held by Native Americans more or less popular at the end of the 20th century than they were at the end of the 19th century? Explain your answer.
18) How does the Native American Great Spirit differ from the Christian god?
19) What place did the warrior have in Native American and European culture?
20) What does "proselytisation" mean?
21) Discuss the upsides and downsides of the 19th century Europeans' confidence in their own culture.
22) Despite all the dangers, the American West held great appeal for many Europeans. Why?
23) Explain "Manifest Destiny".

Maps and Early Explorers

The Whites first settled the east coast, but they didn't stay there for long...

A few Trails crossed the mountains — but they weren't easy

Trails and Mines 1848 - 1874

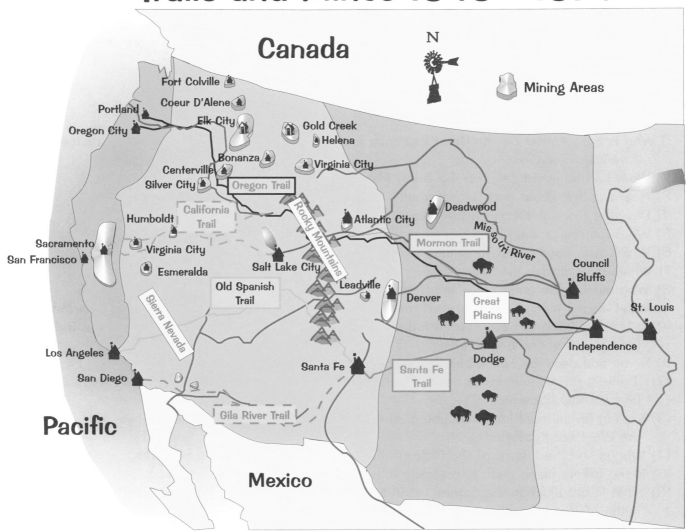

The Trails had been pioneered by Explorers and Trappers

1) The west coast of America first had contact with Europe via Russian traders in the late 1700s. They arrived by sea and traded with the Tlingit Indians.
2) Explorers and trappers had some knowledge of the routes that would later become the Oregon and California trails in the 1840s.

Not learning these maps could coast you dearly...

Another map, with lots more facts to learn. You don't of course have to be able to reproduce these perfectly, but the more routes, places and events you can plot, the more sense all the facts will make when you read them. Turn the page, and try scribbling down the map. It doesn't matter if it looks a pile of tosh — the main thing is to get the bits in the right places relative to each other.

Wagons Roll

People headed West for many different reasons. The journey was very tough.

The Plains were known as the Great American Desert

1) Between would-be settlers in the East and the fertile land in Oregon were The Great Plains.
2) The extremes of climate, sparse rainfall and hard ground meant they were thought unsuitable for agriculture. They were called the Great American Desert.

People went West for many reasons

Many factors influenced people to risk the journey across America. And there needed to be — as many as 10% would die on the journey. The factors can be divided into those pushing them out of the East and those pulling them to the West.

Poverty
Disease
Religious or social persecution
Taxation
Eastern overpopulation

A new start
Fertile cheap land
Government encouragement
Tall tales and newspapers
Gold and silver

There's Gold in Them Thar Hills

1) Miners also went west. The map shows some of the important mining areas. The most famous was that of the California Gold Rush of 1849.
2) Gold was found by James Marshall in 1848. He was working for John Sutter at Sutter's Fort. The news leaked out and soon there were tens of thousands of fortune-seekers coming to California.
3) Some came along the settlers' trails or overland by the Isthmus of Panama (there was no canal there until 1914). Others came by sea round Cape Horn or across the Pacific from China.
4) Some came to run service industries: store keepers, saloon owners, prostitutes — all looking for huge prices for their wares.
5) The first gold was found by panning the stream beds. Most people only came equipped for this method, but the streams were soon exhausted and expensive underground mining took over.
6) Prices of everything were exorbitant, including transport home. Many '49ers had little choice — they could work for mining companies in foul conditions, or starve. A terrible end to a golden dream.
7) Criminals were also attracted to the Gold Rush. There were plenty of con-men, violent thieves and claim jumpers (who stole other people's claims to successful mines). With little formal law enforcement, many townships formed their own miners' courts. They had no permanent prisons, so death sentences were often carried out immediately. There was no right to appeal.

A rush for gold — or just deserts...

There were loads of reasons for heading West. Make sure you can list them, and try to judge how important each was. The California Gold Rush was pretty devastating not only for the area, but for the Native Americans and most of the miners who went there. But it did have benefits too. List the benefits and problems, and decide whether on the whole you think it was a good thing.

The Mormons

Not everyone sought gold or fertile land — the Mormons moved to escape persecution.

The Mormons also travelled West

Farmers and miners weren't the only settlers. A third group were "The Church of Jesus Christ of the Latter Day Saints" — or Mormons. This faith was started by Joseph Smith, who claimed to have seen a vision of an angel called Moroni in 1823. Moroni told Smith to find some gold plates hidden on a hillside. Translations were published in the Book of Mormon in 1830. It told how Jesus had visited America after the Resurrection, and also how three of the lost tribes of Israel had come to America, from which the Indians were descended.

Mormon Beliefs and Practices
Polygamy — A man could have more than one wife.
Proselytisation — Mormons should try to convert other people to their faith.
Politics — Church leaders should seek and be given political power over Mormons and others.
Property — The church held property. There were no rights to individual ownership.
People of God — Obedience would make Mormons God's chosen people in Heaven and on Earth.

The Mormons were persecuted for their religion

Many aspects of the Mormons' faith didn't go down so well with other Americans:
1) Polygamy was seen as scandalous. Many thought it was as bad as slavery.
2) Their efforts to convert people raised fears of rapid expansion and annoyed non-converts.
3) Political aspirations threatened non-believers with religiously inspired legislation.
4) Mormons raised an army and police (the Danites) and there was violence against dissenters.
5) Claims to be the chosen ones of God made the Mormons seem arrogant.
6) Individual ownership is pivotal to American culture. Ironically, working as a community made them wealthy — and this also annoyed non-Mormons.

They were driven out of place after place

Temple at Kirtland

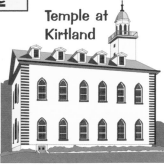

1) The Mormons first settled in Kirtland, Ohio, 1831-7. Violence included J. Smith being tarred and feathered (1832). Their first temple was built here in 1833. The Mormon bank collapsed in 1837 and they were finally driven out to Missouri.
2) In Missouri the Mormons' anti-slavery stance annoyed slave-owners. The Danites were suspected of plotting with Indians. Many of the leaders were arrested — but Brigham Young emerged to lead the Mormons to Illinois.
3) Nauvoo (now Commerce), Illinois — A Charter, given by the governor, allowed Mormons an army and laws. Smith declared Presidential candidacy. In June 1844 Joseph Smith and his brother Hyrum were arrested for the destruction of a dissident printing press. Later that month the jail was attacked by an angry mob of non-Mormons, who killed both brothers.
4) Some factions then left the Mormons, but 15,000 remained when Brigham Young took over.

Learn those five Ps — or it could prove expensive...

The episode of the Mormons is an important chapter in American history, so don't ignore it. The trouble is there's lots of facts to learn. The most important thing is to understand the basic features of their religion (make sure you can list those Ps), and why these and their actions led to their persecution. Write a brief summary of the page — an ideal way to learn it.

The Mormons

Map of the Routes taken by the Mormons

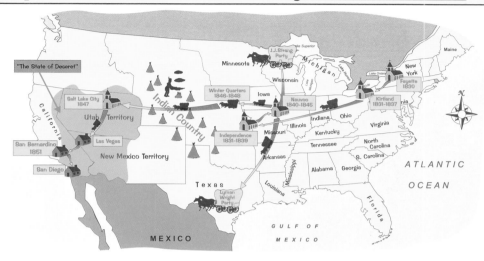

Temple at Salt Lake City

The Mormons settled in Salt Lake Valley

1) Preparations for a move from Nauvoo began in 1845.
2) Anti-Mormon violence increased in 1846. An advance party left to set up winter quarters on the banks of the Missouri River at Platte River Junction. They planted crops to feed Mormons on the journey.
3) In 1847 Young led the Mormons across the Great Plains along Platte River. They were organised like an army but deaths still occurred.
4) They reached Salt Lake Valley on 23 July. Young picked this place despite the harsh conditions. Mormon propaganda suggested the area was geographically similar to Israel.

With much hard work they built Salt Lake City

1) Irrigation work was needed to make things grow. Strict discipline made team work effective.
2) Building work started almost immediately. Young called the area "Deseret". He wanted it to become a Mormon state, independent of the USA and reaching to the Pacific at San Diego.
3) The first crops were destroyed by a plague of grasshoppers. Despite this more Mormons were encouraged to come to Deseret. Increased numbers were needed for success.
4) In 1848 Salt Lake Valley was handed over by Mexico and became Utah, a territory of the USA. It had no access to the sea and no independence, but Young became governor.
5) The Mormons ignored US laws. The Danites suppressed opposition and attacked US officials.
6) In 1857 the US appointed a non-Mormon governor, who arrived with 2500 US troops. Later that year 140 non-Mormon settlers were massacred at Mountain Meadows. The Mormons blamed the Indians, but others suspected the Danites. A Mormon was executed 20 years later for his part in the massacre.
7) Utah wasn't allowed to become a state while it still practised polygamy. The US government stepped up its efforts after Brigham Young's death in 1877, until the Mormons finally abandoned the practice in 1890. Utah was made a state in 1896.

A people taken with a pinch of salt...

Reaching Salt Lake was far from the end of their story. Think of the reasons for their success — what aspects of their beliefs helped them, and which hindered them. Remember that Brigham Young had further plans, which were thwarted by the US government. His dreams of "Deseret" fell by the wayside, and they had to abandon the practise of polygamy to become a state.

Maps and Dates

Time for some politics, I'm afraid. The US government was a key factor in many episodes of the American West's history, so you probably ought to know a bit about it.

1) Map of USA Showing Treaties gaining lands

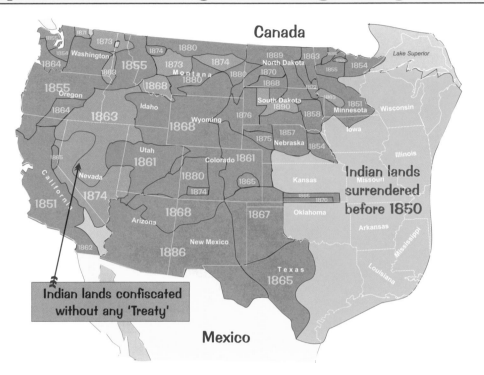

2) Map of USA showing Dates of Statehood

Government for the People

America is a democracy. For too long the majority of White Americans either didn't care about the Native Americans or actually supported genocidal policies. Greed drove them to steal land.

The United States has a Federal Government of States

1) Each State has a Governor and a legislature (law-making body). It sends delegates to the House of Representatives and the Senate in Washington.
2) Laws can be different in different states and areas. This allowed criminals to move from state to state to avoid conviction.

A Territory with 60,000 could become a State

1) As the west developed it was carved up roughly into territories. This is why the borders of the western states are much straighter than those of the eastern ones.
2) Territories with more than 5,000 free male residents could elect some officials — but the federal government appointed many of the more important ones.
3) A territory could become a state when it reached a population of 60,000. Ambitious local politicians often encouraged people to move to their territory for this reason.
4) By 1890 the west had developed so much that the U.S. Bureau of the Census declared the frontier closed (removed). America was no longer divided between East and West.

Different Courts and Lawmen had different jurisdictions

1) Many town marshals only controlled law enforcement in a small area around their town.
2) Federal marshals could enforce laws throughout America — but the crimes had to be those dealt with by the federal courts.
3) The Federal courts try different types of case to the state courts. The final point of appeal for the states is the state governor — not the federal courts.
4) The election of local officials made jobs like town sheriff and judge political. These posts were frequently drawn into the violent disputes of the "Western Civil War of Incorporation"

Gold, Beef and Oil fed growth of America

1) Only a few of the people who struggled into the West for the gold rushes and the Beef Bonanza (page 18) succeeded in making huge fortunes.
2) Gold revenues helped pay for the trans-continental railways and the development of Western cities like San Francisco.
3) Trading in gold with foreign countries made America a major world trading nation.
4) Many of the famous family empires like the Rockefellers date their rise to fortune to our period of study. Oil became important in the last quarter of the 19th century. Many of America's best oil fields are in the West.

Know your unions — or you'll be in a sorry state...

The government was pretty important, so it's pretty important you know a bit about it, and how it was organised. Remember to always think about the facts you're learning. Question things. Was the system of federal and state government the best way to control the West, for instance... But whatever you do, make sure you know the difference between federal and state government.

Treaties with the Indians

Major Indian Treaties and Government Bills

- 1838 Cherokee Treaty (Trail of Tears)
- 1851 1st Fort Laramie Treaty (12,000 people attended)
- 1854 Mormon Cow incident ends Fort Laramie Treaty
- 1861 Fort Wise Treaty — Cheyenne give up land around Denver
- 1865 1st Comanche Reservation Treaty
- 1867 Medicine Creek Treaty — 2nd Comanche reservation treaty
- 1868 2nd Fort Laramie Treaty — end of Red Cloud's War
- 1871 Indian Appropriation Bill
- 1871 Government stops making treaties — new agreements less permanent
- 1887 Allotment Act — reservations carved up into individual family plots — many sold cheap to whites
- 1890 "Closure" of frontier

Greed and the changing West made treaties fail

1) Before <u>1840</u> the whole West seemed like a vast, <u>inhospitable wilderness</u>. The "<u>Permanent Indian Frontier</u>" seemed easy to accept. No-one wanted the <u>Great American Desert</u>.

2) <u>1843</u> saw the beginning of the great migration to <u>Oregon and California</u>. The Whites needed to <u>cross</u> the Plains. There was some disruption to herds, but on the whole this meant <u>opportunities</u> of trade for the Indians.

3) From <u>1848</u> <u>gold</u> was discovered in the West. Previously <u>unwanted land</u> which the Whites were happy to leave to the Indians could suddenly become the <u>most desirable</u> land on the continent.

4) Realisation of the potential of the <u>Great Plains</u> in the <u>1850s</u> and the <u>expanding population</u> of the East made <u>homesteading</u> (the setting up of homes) on the Plains impossible to stop.

5) The <u>clash of cultures</u> made peaceful coexistence an impossible dream. Conflict was <u>inevitable</u>.

6) In <u>1871</u> the <u>Indian Appropriations Bill</u> removed the <u>nation status</u> of the Indians, originally established by the <u>Fort Stanwix Treaty</u> of <u>1768</u>. This made all Indians wards of the US government, making it easier for the <u>Railway companies</u> to acquire reservation lands.

A "Western Civil War of Incorporation" — or just lawlessness?

1) <u>Wyatt Earp</u> and the Clantons, <u>Billy the Kid</u> and Pat Garrett, Jesse James and the <u>Pinkerton Detective Agency</u> have all been represented as both "goodies" and "baddies" in contemporary and modern <u>fiction</u>.

2) The violence in the <u>1870s</u>, <u>80s</u> and <u>90s</u> in the American West were partly due to <u>changes</u> in society. Cattle barons, railroads and other <u>corporations</u> were taking over from the homesteaders, small ranchers and prospector miners. Some historians call the violence the "<u>Western Civil War of Incorporation</u>".

3) This is why many of the <u>outlaws</u> were treated as <u>heroes</u> by some. In some communities it made it impossible for big businesses to get <u>convictions</u>.

Billy 'The Kid'

Treaties — useful for golf in a forest...

The history of the US government's treaties with the Indians is a sorry tale indeed. Many of them were <u>deliberate frauds</u> carried out by cynical land grabbers. But even when the negotiators were acting in good faith, the <u>actions of others</u> or <u>changing circumstances</u> led to breaches of agreements. Now <u>learn those treaties</u> — and check you know them by <u>scribbling</u> them down.

The Wild West

<u>Lawlessness</u> was a big problem in the West. Many people took it into their <u>own hands</u>.

Lack of law enforcement led to <u>Vigilante</u> groups

1) Early on the lack of any <u>formal law enforcement</u> meant that <u>vigilante</u> groups were needed in places, like the miners courts in the Gold rush <u>boom towns</u>.
2) Later on vigilante groups were largely a tool of <u>big business</u>. They were used when legal means failed, for example to suppress the "outlaw" groups opposing the <u>expansion</u> of their empires.
3) Under these circumstances justice, legality, good and evil became very <u>subjective concepts</u> — lawmen and criminals were often very hard to tell apart.

The <u>Johnson County War</u> — a vigilante raid in <u>1892</u>

1) Small-land owners in <u>Johnson County</u> felt that the <u>cattle barons</u> were stealing their <u>land</u>. Ranchers thought that the <u>homesteaders</u> were rustling (stealing) their <u>cattle</u>.
2) In <u>1889</u> a rancher called <u>A.J. Bothwell</u> wanted land claimed by a storekeeper called <u>James Averill</u>. Averill lived with a prostitute called <u>Ella Watson</u> who had some cows that she had <u>rebranded</u>. Bothwell accused them both of <u>rustling</u> and a <u>lynch mob</u> murdered Watson and Averill in front of their cabin.
3) In <u>1892</u> the <u>Wyoming Stock Growers Association</u> hired gunmen and drew up a hit list of 70 names. They mounted a huge vigilante raid into <u>Johnson County</u>, calling themselves the "<u>Regulators</u>". The <u>Union Pacific Railroad</u> kindly laid on a special train for them.
4) The Regulators killed two alleged rustlers, <u>Nate Champion</u> and <u>Nick Ray</u>, but a big <u>posse</u> of locals came out of <u>Buffalo</u> and laid siege to the "<u>invaders</u>" at a ranch called the <u>TA</u>.
5) More locals gathered, including <u>Buffalo's sheriff</u>, until there were about <u>250</u> men ready to kill the Regulators. The <u>Stock Growers Association</u> had influence with the <u>government</u> via the <u>Republican Party</u> and the <u>President</u>. They used this to call out the <u>Army</u>, who rescued the Regulators in a bloodless truce. Despite the efforts of the locals <u>no prosecutions</u> resulted.

<u>Wyatt Earp</u> became a <u>lawman</u> despite a dodgy past

1) Born in <u>1848</u>, <u>Wyatt Earp</u> was arrested in <u>1871</u> for <u>rustling</u> (horse stealing). However he escaped, and the <u>federal system</u> did nothing to prevent his later career as a <u>lawman</u>.
2) He was a natural recruit for the forces of <u>incorporation</u> as he was a keen <u>entrepreneur</u> as well as an effective <u>gunman</u>.
3) He, his <u>brothers</u> and <u>Doc Holliday</u> killed two <u>McLaurys</u> and a <u>Clanton</u> at the <u>OK Corral</u> on <u>26 October 1881</u>. The dead men were typical of the small ranchers/outlaws who opposed, with some <u>popular support</u>, the growth of big business in the West. A <u>bloody feud</u> followed.
4) As <u>victor</u>, Wyatt Earp not only <u>wrote the history</u> of the OK Corral, but got to write the <u>screenplay</u> as well — he worked as an advisor on the early <u>Hollywood westerns</u> before he died in <u>1929</u>.

Wyatt Earp

Learn it or lose marks — it's Earp to you...

Make sure you understand the <u>reasons</u> for all the <u>problems and conflicts</u> — and <u>why</u> vigilante groups arose. Remember that backing up arguments with <u>examples</u> is essential in the Exams, so you really do need to <u>learn those facts</u>. You know the drill — turn the page and <u>scribble</u>...

Revision Summary for Sections 3-4

More questions now, I'm afraid. Don't forget though that if you haven't looked back at the previous questions already, then it's about time you did. You really do have to keep going over stuff like this if you want it to stick in that head of yours. You should really go over these questions till you can reel off those answers — just like that. When you can do that, you'll know you know it.

1) What factors made early migrants want to cross America?
2) By what name were the Great Plains also known in the 1840s?
3) Who first discovered gold in California?
4) Describe the routes taken by '49ers to get to California.
5) Which Californian city and port was mostly built because of the Gold Rush?
6) What was the most common technique used by prospectors to find gold? How did it work?
7) This technique only worked for the early arrivals. Why? What choice faced many of the later arrivals because of this?
8) Why was everything so expensive in California?
9) How did the expectations of the '49ers compare with reality?
10) Who kept law and order in the boom towns?
11) In what ways did: a) all Americans b) a small minority, benefit from the Gold Rush?
12) What is the full name of the Mormon faith and who founded it?
13) What did the Mormon leader claim to have found hidden on a hillside?
14) How did he know where to make his discovery?
15) Who are the Native Americans descended from according to the Book of Mormon?
16) Describe the aspects of the Mormon faith that were unpopular with most other Americans.
17) Who were the Danites?
18) Why were the Mormons' founder and his brother arrested just before their deaths?
19) How did the church's founder die?
20) Who replaced him as leader?
21) Which river did the Mormons follow west?
22) What preparations did they make to ease their journey?
23) Why did the Mormons decide to settle in the Salt Lake Valley?
24) Describe the difficulties of the first few seasons in Salt Lake City.
25) What happened at Mountain Meadows?
26) What insect was a problem for many settlers in the West, including the Mormons?
27) What is a federal government?
28) How did a territory become a state?
29) To whom do people on "Death Row" make their final appeal?
30) Which three commodities produced by the West were most important in building America?
31) Which treaty recognised the nation status of the Indians? Which bill removed it?
32) Why is the violence in the West between 1870 and 1900 sometimes called "The Western Civil War of Incorporation"?
33) Who controlled the vigilante group involved in the Johnson County War of 1892?
34) For what crime was Wyatt Earp a wanted man?
35) How did Wyatt Earp and the Gunfight at the O.K. Corral fit into the Western Civil War of Incorporation?

Maps and Dates

The coming of the <u>railways</u> brought <u>opportunities</u> — to move West or to sell your cattle.

Map Showing Stage Coach Routes and Railways

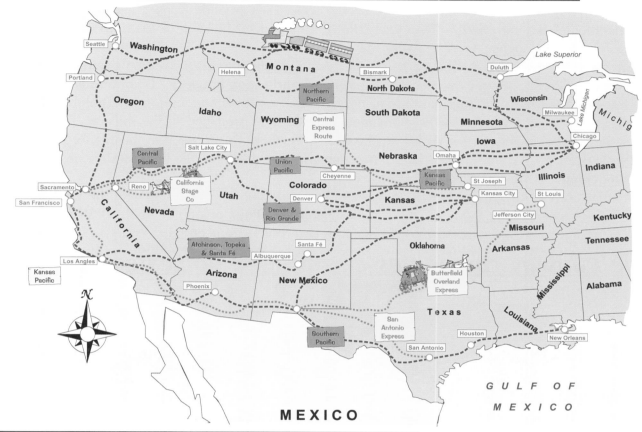

Map Showing the big Cattle Trails

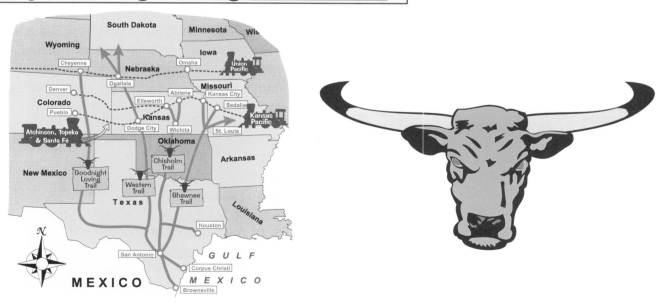

Train your mind — and rattle off those railways...

More maps, and you know how to <u>learn them</u>. Don't forget to <u>look back</u> over the stuff you've already done from time to time. Even if you know it now, you'll <u>soon forget it</u> if you don't go back over it. So review stuff <u>regularly</u> — and <u>scribble it down</u> to be sure you know it...

Homesteaders and the Railways

The US government did a lot to encourage homesteaders and the building of the railways.

Homesteaders set up homes (homesteads) on the Plains

1) In the 1850s some homesteaders were on the Low Plains (mostly Kansas and Nebraska).
2) Conditions were very hard. There was little or no wood for building or fuel. The land was too hard for light ploughs. Lack of water made crops like maize fail. Wind and extremes of climate battered, froze and baked people in turn. Grasshopper plagues often destroyed crops.
3) People made do. Houses were made of clods of earth (sod houses). Dried buffalo dung and cow-pats were used as fuel, and recycling produced an American icon — the patchwork quilt.
4) Much of the land being taken by homesteaders was land promised to the Indians. The writers of the treaties had seen the Plains as the Great American Desert — they hadn't foreseen the demand there would be for the land. This demand would have made it impossible, in a democracy, to live up to the treaties.
5) A small number of Indians took to homesteading and filed for land along with the Whites. In 1869 some Santee Sioux established the Flandreau Sioux colony in South Dakota. Most Indians though found themselves forced more and more into a corner.

The Railway companies encouraged homesteading

1) Politicians and the railway companies were keen to encourage homesteading.
2) In 1862 the companies were granted large areas of land (increased 1864) to help fund the railways. They sold land cheap to homesteaders. They wanted customers for trains.
3) Politicians wanted 60,000 residents in their territory so it could become a state.
4) Companies and politicians made exaggerated claims about the good life on the Plains.
5) Economic, geographical and engineering problems were faced. The government supplied loans. Labour shortages were solved by using Chinese workers. Indians attacked railway gangs.
6) Railway lines built from the East and West finally met at Promontory, Utah, in May 1869. This made migration to the West very much easier, and improved communication with the East.

A government Act and new Technology helped too

1) The Homestead Act of 1862 gave each settler 160 acres of free land.
2) New crops were tried, including Turkey Red Wheat from Russia. Better machinery was also developed, including John Deere's "Sodbuster" plough. Wind pumps increased water supply and farmers learnt "dry farming".
3) In many areas farmers needed more than 160 acres to make a decent living. The Timber Culture Act (1873) and the Desert Land Act (1877) gave them more land for free or at low cost.
4) Many of the settlers were not Anglo-Americans from the East. Immigrants from all over Europe were coming to America. African Americans had begun to move west after their emancipation (release) during the Civil War.
5) New techniques allowed the High Plains to be settled. Despite many tales of extreme suffering, the Great Plains were emerging as the "Breadbasket" of the nation.
6) 430,000 settlers had filed claims in Kansas, Nebraska and the Dakotas by the end of 1895.

The Beef Bonanza and Cattle Trails

The cattle trade made good money for some, but it led to many clashes.

The Beef Bonanza led to the great Cattle Trails

1) Open ranching of cattle started in Mexico, which also included Texas until 1836.
2) Texas rebelled against Mexican rule in 1836, and entered the USA in 1840. Many Mexicans were driven out, leaving their cattle to Anglo-American ranchers.
3) The Anglo-Americans brought their own cattle with them, some descended from English Longhorns. Their cattle interbred with Mexican Criollos cattle to produce the most famous breed in the world — the Texas Longhorn.
4) Increased popularity of beef in the 1850s made it worthwhile to drive cattle to the eastern markets, but the real Beef Bonanza and the great trails awaited two more factors — the American Civil War and the railways.

5) Many Texans left their ranches to fight for the South in the Civil War. Whilst away their cattle continued to breed. Charles Goodnight left 180 cattle in 1860, but returned in 1865 to find he owned 5,000.
6) As the railways spread across the Plains men like Joseph McCoy (the original "Real McCoy") saw money to be made in moving beef cattle by rail to the eastern cities and Indian reservations. McCoy built up the cattle town Abilene on the Kansas Pacific Railroad. Ranchers like Oliver Loving and Charles Goodnight blazed trails to the railway cattle towns — and made fortunes.

Cattlemen and Homesteaders often clashed

1) Longhorn cattle carried a tick which in turn carried a disease called Texas Fever. The tough Longhorns were immune to it but homesteaders' cattle were not. This meant homesteaders often lost cattle when herds were driven across their land.
2) Lack of wood for fences meant early farmsteads were cordoned off by a single ploughed furrow. This wasn't too cow-proof, so many crops were also destroyed by passing herds.
3) From 1874 the invention of barbed wire made stock-proof fencing cheap. Homesteaders fenced their land, reducing cattlemen's access to water and making long cattle drives much harder.

Changing tastes and hard winters ended the Bonanza

1) Some ranches were set up on the Great Plains to reduce the distance that cattle had to be driven. This increased conflict with the homesteaders.
2) The Eastern markets began to demand a higher quality of meat than the Longhorn could provide. Cattle men like John Iliff started crossbreeding them with Herefords — but the new cattle needed more care than could be given on the open range.
3) The herds became too big for the grazing areas. Hard winters also sped up the decline by killing large numbers of cattle (esp. 1886-7). Many cowboys also died.
4) But the decline didn't stop vast commercial empires being built by the cattle barons.

Now learn some facts to beef up your answers...

Although the cattle had to be transported huge distances over land, the railways were still very important for getting the meat to its final destinations. Make sure you know the reasons for the rise and decline of the cattle industry (don't forget the role government played).

The Real Cowboys

We all have a picture of what a cowboy should be like from the famous screen cowboys — John Wayne, Clint Eastwood, Billy Crystal. What were they really like?

The Cowboys were a very mixed bunch

1) Large numbers of cowboys were Mexican or African Americans. Some were ex-soldiers from the Civil War, some were outlaws.
2) Most Cowboys were young and single. They had little time for a family life.
3) A tiny number of women took to ranching in their own right. The Becker sisters ran a ranch in the San Luis Valley in the 1880s.

The cowboy's Job was very tough and badly paid

1) Boredom and discomfort were part of the job. Winters were spent watching the cattle from line camps on the edges of the ranch. Trail life was mostly breathing dust and staring at cows.
2) Great stamina, vigilance and skill were needed, especially during a drive. Longhorn cattle are big and aggressive. Rounding them up and cutting out the correct cattle from mixed herds on the open range took skill. Long days, mostly in the saddle, were followed by nights on watch.
3) Indians often charged a levy for crossing their land. Sometimes Indians and other rustlers would steal or stampede cattle. Diplomacy or guns could be needed.
4) Whilst on the trail the cowboys were highly disciplined as much by each other as by their bosses. They had to work as a team to succeed and there weren't the chances to misbehave.
5) Pay was very low and tended to come in one lump at the end of a drive. Young men at the end of a difficult, boring job with money in their pockets didn't need encouragement to whoop it up. Cow towns like Abilene and Cheyenne grew to provide ample vices and temptations.

What were the tools of the trade?

Pistol — Used to shoot wolves, rustlers and (rarely) in drunken brawls. Pistols like the Colt "Peacemaker" fired brass cartridges. They were more reliable and safer than the "cap and ball" revolvers of the Civil War.

Hat — Broad-brimmed felt hat to give protection from all weathers.

Bandana — Large handkerchief worn around the neck or over the nose and mouth to protect them from dust.

Saddle — Large and with a high pommel and cantle for support — increasing comfort for both rider and horse. The cap on the pommel allows a rope to be tied off.

Horse — The best horse for cowboys was the American Quarter Horse. Sturdy and compact, this breed could manoeuvre well and travel all day.

Chaps — Leather overtrousers that protect the legs from thorns and cattle.

Boots — The high-heeled boot originated in Mexico and helped the feet stay in the stirrups.

Lariat or lasso — used to rope cows, especially during roundups for branding.

Stop horsing around and do some work...

The job of the cowboy provided one of the biggest sources of legend in the American West. The thing is though, the life of a cowboy generally bore very little relation to the legend — very few cowboy films, for instance, actually have any cows in. Think about how and why the legends grew.

Maps and Dates

Long-running disputes between the Indians and Whites finally came to a head in the Indian Wars.

There were many Major Battles on the Plains

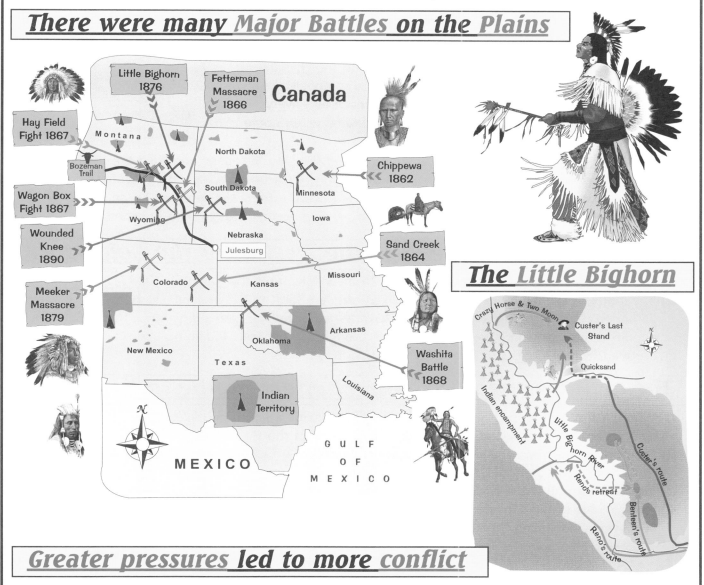

The Little Bighorn

Greater pressures led to more conflict

1) Indian tribes had always fought each other. Feuds developed that could last for generations, although oral history did tend to exaggerate their permanency.

2) Eastern tribes retreated from the Whites, which meant they came into conflict with the western tribes more often. The Sioux only moved onto the Great Plains from the Great Lakes region during the 18th century, when they were effectively forced out by the Whites and the Ojibwas.

3) The Cherokees in the south were forced out of Georgia and Texas in the 1830s, despite having accepted and adapted to many of the settlers' ways. They had taken to settled farming, lived in European-style houses and had produced an alphabet with which they published their own newspaper (the *Phoenix*). The US President Jackson and Texas President Lamar used dodgy land deals, legislation (The Indian Removal Act of 1830) and military action to force them to Oklahoma. Over 2,000 Cherokees died on this "Trail of Tears".

Traditional rivalries — feud have thought of that...

Another very handy map. Make sure you know those battles — turn over the page now and roughly sketch the map. Remember — don't try to draw it accurately. Just scribble it down as fast as you can. You're just checking you know roughly where the battles were.

A New Tribe in the Western Ring — Whites

The Indian Wars broke out in many different places, and involved many tribes.

There was much Strife in the far south west

Olive Oatman gave lecture tours after Mohave captivity

1) The Indians of what are now New Mexico, Arizona and south California had taken part in mutual raiding with the Hispanic Mexicans long before Anglo-Americans began to appear from the north east. Both sides sometimes took captives as slaves. This later produced effective propaganda material when some Anglo-American women and children were taken.

2) The Americans arrived and in the 1830s defeated first the Mexicans and then the Indians. Guerrilla warfare followed. The Apaches and Comanches became legendary, along with leaders like Cochise and Geronimo. The Navajos were effectively defeated by an 1863-64 campaign by Kit Carson. General George Crook successfully fought the Apaches.

The Indian Wars spread to the West after the Gold Rush

1) The Indians in the West had little conflict with the Whites until the California Gold Rush of 1849.

2) The influx of Whites looking for gold had a terrible effect on the Indians. Hunting and gathering were disrupted by the mines, leaving many Indians near starvation. Some fighting occurred, but far worse were the diseases brought by miners. Indian numbers in California dropped from 100,000 in 1846 to 30,000 in 1851.

The Civil War had little direct effect on the Indians

1) Although the American Civil War is thought of as having Eastern and Western campaigns, little happened west of Vicksburg (east of the Great Plains).

2) Some attempts were made by both sides to involve the Indians — to make trouble for the other side.

3) The main effect of the Civil War on our story was the effect on the cattle trade.

4) Many of the soldiers involved in the final stages of the Indian Wars had been in the Civil War — including Custer, Sherman and Sheridan.

Little Crow's War — murder and looting in 1862

1) This campaign showed the worst of both the Whites and Indians.

2) The Santee Sioux had been peaceful, accepting reservation life and adopting the Whites' ways.

3) The Civil War led to shortages, and a poor harvest left Indians near starvation.

4) White officials and traders reacted without compassion, refusing credit and even telling the Indians to eat grass or worse.

5) Four Indians returning from an unsuccessful hunt killed five settlers for a dare.

6) Little Crow, despite initially being for peace, led the Santee Sioux warriors on a murder and looting campaign. It lasted until New Ulm and Fort Ridgely held out.

7) Angry mobs of Whites attacked the Indians who had surrendered. 38 were hanged.

The Indian Wars — hardly civil affairs...

The Indian Wars were a major episode in American West history — and generated much controversy and bitterness still felt today. The US government basically wanted to get rid of the Indians, or at least to get them off most of the land. Make sure you know the reasons why — try making a list, then look back over the book to see if you've missed anything.

Early Conflicts on the Plains

Many Indians wanted peace, but in the end were <u>forced into action</u>.

The <u>Cheyenne</u> Uprising and <u>Sand Creek</u> — 1864

1) <u>Black Kettle's</u> Cheyenne were living on a reservation at <u>Sand Creek</u>, Colorado. They were on the verge of <u>starvation</u>. Black Kettle advocated <u>peace</u>.
2) Warriors from the reservation started <u>raiding</u> the South Platte trails and committed <u>atrocities</u>.
3) Denver public opinion was enraged by a display of the <u>mutilated corpses</u> of a settler family.
4) <u>Major J. Downing</u> attacked a Cheyenne camp at <u>Cedar Bluffs</u>, shouting, "Commence killing!"
5) <u>Colonel J.M. Chivington</u> decided to attack Black Kettle's camp at <u>Sand Creek</u> on <u>29th Nov. 1864</u>. Chivington wanted to <u>exterminate</u> the Indians.
6) Around <u>300</u> Indians were killed — but only a tiny minority were <u>warriors</u>. Women and children were deliberately <u>butchered</u>. Bodies were <u>scalped and mutilated</u>.
7) Even the enraged population of Denver realised that this was well out of order. Chivington <u>resigned</u> but received no other punishment. Black Kettle escaped and continued to try for peace. He was killed in a further village massacre at <u>Washita</u>, Oklahoma in <u>1868</u>. The soldiers this time were led by <u>Lt. Col. George Custer</u>.

Red Cloud's War and the <u>Bozeman Trail</u> — 1866

1) The <u>Bozeman Trail</u> connected the Platte River with the <u>mines</u> in Montana. It passed through the <u>hunting grounds</u> of the Sioux, which had been guaranteed to them by the <u>Fort Laramie Treaty</u> of <u>1851</u>.
2) The army wanted to build <u>forts</u> on the trail to protect travellers from Indians. Talks were held with <u>Red Cloud</u> in <u>1866</u>, one of the Indian leaders. The talks failed when the Indians saw soldiers marching out to begin building <u>before any deal</u> had been struck.
3) <u>Col. H.B. Carrington</u> started building three forts. He was harassed by Indians, including <u>Sitting Bull</u> and <u>Crazy Horse</u>.
4) Several skirmishes occurred outside the forts. Then in December 1866 <u>Capt. W.J. Fetterman's</u> force was ambushed and destroyed. Around 100 soldiers died.

Red Cloud

Sitting Bull

5) Bad weather saved Carrington's force, but the army had to negotiate what was effectively a <u>surrender</u> in <u>April 1868</u>. The forts were abandoned, then burnt by the Indians.
6) In <u>1867</u> the Cheyennes, Comanches, Kiowas and Arapaho accepted the <u>Medicine Lodge Treaty</u>. They agreed to leave their hunting grounds and live permanently in <u>reservations</u>.

I bet Carrington had reservations after that...

The Indian Wars weren't just one war. They were a <u>series</u> of intermittent and localised conflicts, fought against different tribes — not against one united nation. Make sure you remember the <u>key people</u> involved — on both sides. Make a <u>list</u> of them, and make sure you can write a bit about <u>what each of them did</u>. Learn a few <u>dates</u> too — and impress those Examiners.

Reservations and the Little Bighorn

The forcing of Indians into smaller and smaller reservations could not go on indefinitely.

The Reservations — Stopovers on the way to Oblivion

1) The creation of Indian Reservations formed the "Permanent Indian Frontier", which ran along the line of the western borders of Minnesota, Iowa, Missouri, and Arkansas.

2) The sorry tale of the Indian Wars can be simplified to a cycle. White breaches of agreements were followed by Indian uprisings, leading to their military defeat and confinement to smaller reservations. Further breaches then followed, and the cycle repeated.

3) Eventually, the Indians were left without the territory to support themselves. They were reliant on government handouts, which were often supervised by corrupt officials. They were treated with contempt by many of the Whites around them.

4) There were some mitigating factors in favour of the White government and its army. The Indian chiefs didn't control their warriors like an army. Indians continued raiding even if their chiefs had made deals.

5) Raiding was continued by many Indians as it enhanced their status and provided material gain. Total peace was not wanted by many Indians as it was by most Whites.

6) The men of the Plains tribes were hunters and warriors. Once on the reservations, denied access to hunting grounds and not allowed to raid either other tribes or the Whites, they had little to do. Alcoholism became rife and led to revolts and sprees of murderous violence.

7) The Dawes Act in 1887 was designed by the US government to break up tribes, end the Indian way of life and encourage Indians to become 'normal American citizens'. Reservations were broken up into 'allotments' and given out to individual tribe members to own and farm.

8) Any land not claimed by Indians following the Dawes Act was declared 'surplus' and made free to settlers. Within 20 years, two-thirds of the original reservations were in White hands.

The Sioux Campaign (1876) — climax of the Indian Wars

1) In 1874 troops under Lt. Col. George Custer confirmed the presence of gold in the Black Hills of Dakota. The hills were sacred to the Sioux, and had been guaranteed to them by the Fort Laramie Treaty of 1868.

2) Despite government opposition a gold rush started, centring on the town of Deadwood.

3) Sitting Bull and Crazy Horse raised the largest Indian force ever seen (about 4,000 warriors from a population in rebellion of 50,000 — mostly Sioux and Cheyenne).

4) The Army sent to oppose this uprising was led by Gen. George Crook. He was one of the army's best Indian-fighters, and had gained a reputation for dealing fairly with the Indians in negotiations. This campaign was not his best.

5) Crook hoped to split the Indian force but ended up splitting his own instead. This error was worsened by the ambition and glory hunting of Custer (commanding the 7th Cavalry), who deliberately sought the chance to attack the Indians alone.

6) Custer was outnumbered more than 5 to 1 as he entered the valley of the Little Bighorn. He didn't even have the advantage of technology — many of the Indians were armed with repeating Winchester rifles, while Custer's soldiers had single-shot Springfields.

7) Custer and all 225 of his command were killed. The army and the government wanted revenge, but the Indians were defeated by the weather and the loss of many horses.

8) The destruction of the buffalo herds (the "Great Plains Massacre") and the killing of ponies during campaigns had been two of the Whites' most effective weapons in the Indian Wars.

Prophets of White Destruction

A string of Native American prophets or messiahs emerged to tell of glorious renewals of Indian fortunes and the destruction of the Whites.

Nez Percé Campaign — Chief Joseph's Retreat, 1877

1) In 1863 the government had started to pressurise the peaceful Nez Percé Indians of Idaho and Oregon to sign treaties giving up much of their land. Two generations of chiefs, both called Joseph, negotiated intelligently and peacefully against these treaties.
2) In 1876 negotiations had stalled. The Dreamer Cult of Smohalla called for the extermination of the Whites. War became unavoidable when 20 settlers were killed by some drunken Indians.
3) Chief Joseph fought a masterly retreat into Idaho and Montana, notable for its relative lack of atrocities against civilians. He surrendered on 5th October 1877.

Chato and Geronimo led a campaign from Mexico

1) In 1881 a shaman called Nakaidoklini said his medicine could raise dead warriors and clear the Whites from Arizona.
2) This led to a revolt by reservation Apaches and a mutiny by Apache army scouts on 30th August 1881. There followed a very cruel cross-border campaign led by Chato and the non-chief Geronimo. It was only defeated by cooperation between the US and Mexican governments in 1883 and 1884. The main Army officers involved were Gens. Crook and Miles.
3) Several more outbreaks of Indian violence occurred, some fuelled by alcohol. Geronimo surrendered for the final time on 4th Sept. 1886.

Geronimo

Ghost Dancers and Wounded Knee — 29th Dec. 1890

Big Foot killed at Wounded Knee

1) The seer Wovoka taught that a special Ghost Dance could raise the dead and bring a new world free from the Whites. He was opposed to violence, but his teachings were taken as a call for war.
2) Sitting Bull had retreated into Canada after the 1876 campaign. He joined Buffalo Bill's Wild West Show in 1885, but soon returned to the reservation. He was killed in a bungled attempt to arrest him on 15th Dec. 1890. The government wrongly thought he was a leader of the Ghost Dance movement.
3) Big Foot of the Sioux had camped at Wounded Knee to avoid the trouble that was brewing.
4) Troops caught up with him and tried to disarm the Sioux. Fighting broke out after a single shot was fired by one of the troops. It went down in history as the Battle of Wounded Knee.
5) Some 150 Sioux and 25 soldiers died. Most of the Sioux were women and children.

The end of the wars — and Sioux long to a way of life...

The Wounded Knee massacre was the last major "battle" of the Indian Wars, and the American government had got its way. Think about the reasons for their victory — in particular, was it just down to their greater numbers... See if you can describe the roles played by each of the following on each side: deception, mistrust, revenge, emotion and bad discipline.

Pulp Fiction and Wild West Shows

Myths and legends of the American West grew rapidly, even as the events were happening.

Early "Travel Writers" and Painters Blazed the Way

1) Accounts of the American West appealed to the public. They began to generate a mythology even before our period of study. Zebulon Pike (1810) and Lewis and Clark (1814) published accounts of expeditions in the West.

2) In the 1830s painters like George Catlin and Karl Bodmer were travelling into the West and painting from life. Their interpretations appear again and again as illustrations of "authentic" Native Americans.

Dime novels fictionalised events before the smoke cleared

1) Dime novels (the original "pulp fiction") became popular at just the right time to glamorise the American west — from the Indian Wars to the Western Civil War of Incorporation.

2) Some writers followed their "real-life" heroes about the country, exaggerating their feats and often making up new ones when the real events ran out. Ned Buntline followed the exploits of William F. Cody — otherwise known as Buffalo Bill.

3) People even started to write about their own "real-life" adventures. A largely fictional account of the life of Billy the Kid was written by Pat Garrett, the man who killed him.

4) The Western Civil War of Incorporation generated propaganda that flooded into western dime novel fiction. Films based on early novels include "Pat Garrett and Billy the Kid", "Butch Cassidy and the Sundance Kid", "Shane", "The Virginian" and "The Gunfight at the OK Corral". Characters were simplistically cast as either "goodies" or "baddies". Some adapted real events and people — others were pure fiction.

Wild West Shows mixed Fact and Fantasy

1) The most famous Wild West Show was that of Buffalo Bill, an ex-army scout. The show started in 1883 as the "Wild West, Rocky Mountain, and Prairie Exhibition".

2) Buffalo Bill's cast included Sitting Bull and performers like Annie Oakley, famed for her shooting skills.

3) The image presented was a glitzy fantasy. Life stories of the cast were adapted to fit the mythology of the show.

4) During one of his British tours Buffalo Bill presented, as a gift, a Lakota Sioux Ghost Dance shirt taken from the site of the Wounded Knee massacre. It was kept in a Glasgow museum until returned to Dakota in 1998 amid talk of "repatriation".

The Wild West — that's a novel idea...

The American West is a very hard period to study because our view of it today is badly obscured by the myth and legend that has grown around it. The image of the American West became a core part of America's self-image and influences the way America functions today. Make sure you understand why the myths and legends developed, and why they were so popular.

Hollywood and TV

Twentieth century <u>technology</u> has allowed the further growth of <u>Western mythology</u>.

Cinema and Television keep the fantasy alive

1) The "<u>goodies and baddies</u>" characters of the dime novels, lots of <u>action</u> and <u>simple plots</u> made the "<u>Western</u>" a hit for the film industry. Like the Wild West shows some early films used <u>genuine historical characters</u> to add authenticity to their stories. <u>Wyatt Earp</u> was the most famous western character to work in the film industry.

2) Fictional western characters have influenced the real world. <u>John Wayne</u> made several films and tours to inspire <u>American troops</u> in the Second World War, the Korean War and Vietnam. <u>Ronald Reagan</u> and <u>Clint Eastwood</u> had political careers after playing western characters.

3) When looking at the "<u>Code of the West</u>" it's often hard to separate fact from fiction. Manslaughter was generally excused if there'd been a "<u>fair fight</u>". American <u>common law</u> still differs from British in that there's no obligation for someone to <u>run away</u> if they can, rather than <u>fight</u> to defend themselves. However the "<u>high-noon walkdown</u>" with holstered pistols rarely if ever happened.

4) Modern Westerns like "<u>Dances with Wolves</u>" (<u>1990</u>) and "<u>Unforgiven</u>" (<u>1992</u>) are in some ways <u>more realistic</u> than earlier films. This can be more <u>confusing</u> though, for all films aim to tell a <u>good story</u>. By picking only the exciting bits and <u>exaggerating</u> "true stories", we can be misled more than if they were more obviously <u>fiction</u>.

The Western fantasy draws on many other traditions

1) <u>Hollywood</u> used themes from many <u>other genres</u> (types of story) to build the cinema <u>western tradition</u>. Sometimes it even took stories whole and redressed them as westerns.

2) "<u>The Magnificent Seven</u>" (<u>1960</u>) is a very famous western, but it is really a resetting of a Japanese film called "<u>The Seven Samurai</u>" directed by <u>Akira Kurosawa</u> (<u>1954</u>).

3) <u>Robin Hood</u> influenced many of the westerns which have a <u>criminal hero</u>.

4) The <u>lone rider</u> cowboy/gunfighter hero harks back to the errant knights of <u>Arthurian</u> legend.

The Western fantasy has lots of stereotypes

1) The vast majority of Western heroes are presented as <u>White Anglo-Saxon males</u>.

2) Other <u>immigrant</u> groups, whether Germanic, Latin American or African, tend to be cast in "colourful" <u>bit parts</u>.

3) The fantasy is totally <u>schizophrenic</u> about <u>Native Americans</u>. They're either <u>heathen, drunken savages</u> or <u>noble savages</u> with arcane powers. Many films with major <u>Indian characters</u> used White actors e.g. <u>Burt Lancaster</u> in "<u>Apache</u>" (<u>1954</u>).

Film me in — I think I'm losing the plot...

It's important you understand the <u>effects</u> films and other media have had on the <u>original stories</u> — how they've added to the mythology. The key is <u>money</u> — the films were all made to make money, and so an <u>appealing plot</u> is a lot more important than the <u>truth</u>. Think what images you've seen in films and documentaries, and <u>why</u> they're less likely to be reliable than <u>historians</u>.

Revision Summary for Sections 5-7

The last page of Western questions. Don't forget to go through these regularly — and make sure you can do them all. And if you can do these, get hold of some of those ghastly Exam questions. After all, they're the ones that count. You know it makes sense...

1) What made homesteading on the Plains so difficult?
2) What were the special features of "dry farming"?
3) Discuss three technological advances that helped Plains homesteaders.
4) Wood was scarce on the Plains. Give three uses for wood and explain the alternative(s) used by homesteaders.
5) Why did the railway companies encourage homesteading?
6) How did the railway companies solve their labour problems?
7) Discuss the ethnic mix of Plains homesteaders.
8) Where and when was the East-West rail link finally completed?
9) What event led to the breeding of the Texas Longhorn?
10) What happened to the cattle population of Texas during the Civil War?
11) Name one man who benefited from the change in cattle population and explain how he cashed in on his good fortune.
12) What piece of technology allowed for the great cattle drives and the Beef Bonanza?
13) Who made his fortune by building up Abilene? What was special about Abilene?
14) Discuss the reasons for conflict between cattlemen and homesteaders.
15) What was "Texas Fever"? Why was it a problem for homesteaders but not cattlemen?
16) How did John Iliff change the cattle business?
17) Would you really like to be a cowboy or cowgirl? Discuss.
18) What special features of the American Quarter Horse made it especially suited to being a cowboy's mount?
19) Why was the "Peacemaker" a better pistol than the "Dragoon" carried during the Civil War?
20) Outline at least three factors that brought an end to the long trail drives of the Beef Bonanza.
21) To what extent was there peace on the Plains before the arrival of the Whites?
22) How had the Cherokees tried to fit into European ways in Georgia and Texas, and how were they repaid?
23) Why did Indian numbers in California drop from 100,000 in 1846 to 30,000 in 1851?
24) Discuss the medium- and short-term causes of the Santee Sioux War of 1862.
25) Describe the events at Sand Creek on 29th November 1864 and what led to them.
26) Custer wasn't the only officer to get his soldiers and himself massacred by underestimating the Indians. Name another and describe the circumstances.
27) Why was the Bozeman Trail important to: a) the Indians? b) the Whites?
28) The Second Fort Laramie Treaty of 1868 amounted to the army's surrender to Red Cloud. Describe the events leading to this rare Indian victory.
29) Why was reservation life so bad for the Indians?
30) Name two northern tribes and two southern tribes involved in the Indian Wars.
31) Who commanded the army forces in the Sioux campaign of 1876?
32) What happened at the Little Bighorn?
33) Name three cavalry commanders who learnt their trade in the Civil War.
34) What effect did the Civil War have on the Indians and the treatment of the Indians by the Whites?
35) Compare the Ghost Dance cult of Wovoka with the similar cult of the 1870s and 80s.
36) Were the events at Wounded Knee on 29th December 1890 a battle, massacre or an act of incompetence?
37) Pick a cowboy film and discuss its relationship to some of the factual events you've studied.

American West Index

American West Index

Important Dates

Here's an example of a <u>timeline</u> — a handy way to show the <u>order</u> of important events.

Critical events and Turning points

BC

3000 — Writing

1380 — Minoan Crete destroyed

460 — Hippocratic Corpus

0

476 — Fall of Rome

663 — Synod of Whitby

1200

1348 — Black Death

1400s — Law of Edgar revoked

1454 — Printing in Europe

1660 — Founding of Royal Society

1665 — Great Plague of London

1720 — Inoculation in Britain

1796 — First vaccination

1831 — Cholera in Britain

1842 — Chadwick Report

1845 — 1st Public Health Act

1846/7 — Ether and Chloroform in use

1854 — Cholera linked to water pollution (Snow)

1857 — Germ Theory (Pasteur)

1875 — 2nd Public Health Act

1890 — Antiseptic in general use

1895 — First X-rays

1896 — Becquerel discovers radioactivity

1900 — Blood groups discovered

1906 — Liberal Reforms

1928 — Penicillin (Fleming)

1939 - 45 — World War II

1951 — First kidney transplant

1953 — Structure of DNA identified

Late 1950s — The Pill

1981 — AIDS discovered

AD

Egyptian culture

Roman culture

Greek culture

MONGOL EMPIRE

Arab Empire

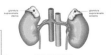

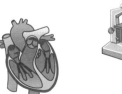
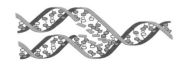

Important People

People, people — where would we be without them?

The most important people

Thousands and thousands of people have contributed to the development of medicine. We've mentioned quite a few in this book — but some were more influential than others. Here are the birthdays of some of them. You should be able to say what contribution each of them made to medicine. For many you should know enough to be able to write a short essay on their work and contribution — and you could be asked to in the Exam.

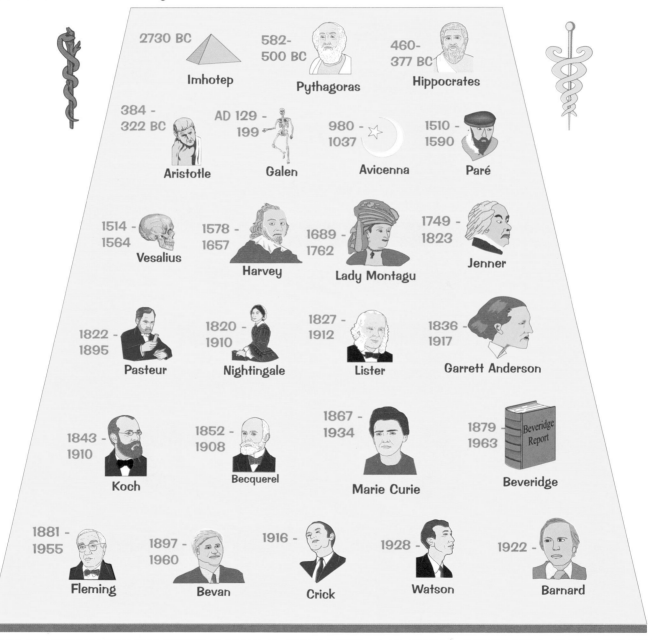

2730 BC — Imhotep

582-500 BC — Pythagoras

460-377 BC — Hippocrates

384 - 322 BC — Aristotle

AD 129 - 199 — Galen

980 - 1037 — Avicenna

1510 - 1590 — Paré

1514 - 1564 — Vesalius

1578 - 1657 — Harvey

1689 - 1762 — Lady Montagu

1749 - 1823 — Jenner

1822 - 1895 — Pasteur

1820 - 1910 — Nightingale

1827 - 1912 — Lister

1836 - 1917 — Garrett Anderson

1843 - 1910 — Koch

1852 - 1908 — Becquerel

1867 - 1934 — Marie Curie

1879 - 1963 — Beveridge (Beveridge Report)

1881 - 1955 — Fleming

1897 - 1960 — Bevan

1916 - — Crick

1928 - — Watson

1922 - — Barnard

Themes are a factor life — so don't bypass them...

These pages are probably the most important in the book. Exams love to ask about the themes and factors — so think about them as you read the other sections. That way you'll spot more connections — and that'll help you remember more. The same goes for causes, consequences, change and continuity. Reread this section from time to time to keep it fresh in your mind.

MEDICINE THROUGH TIME INTRODUCTION

Archaeology and Medicine

OK, time to get down to the details. Prehistory's when it all started.

Prehistory *is the time before written records*

Prehistory is defined as the time <u>before written records</u>, which means that it ended at different times for different societies. Some societies are <u>still</u> in prehistory, as they don't yet have <u>writing</u>.

> Although we can never be totally sure what life was like in prehistory (or history for that matter), combining different sorts of evidence can allow us to make a good guess.

Archaeology *can tell us a lot about prehistoric people*

1) <u>Cave paintings</u> and other prehistoric artwork indicate that prehistoric people believed in a <u>spiritual world</u>. It's likely that their <u>explanations</u> of illness would be based on <u>evil spirits</u>, and illnesses would require <u>spiritual or religious</u> cures.

2) Archaeology also tells us that our prehistoric ancestors were mostly <u>nomadic hunter-gatherers</u>, although <u>agriculture</u> developed before the earliest written records. Hunter-gatherers lived in <u>small extended family</u> groups and moved from place to place following game and looking for edible plants and other resources.

3) <u>Social organisation</u> probably didn't extend much beyond <u>family structures</u>, even after the invention of agriculture. <u>Special projects</u> like Stonehenge must have involved large numbers. These probably came together when <u>food</u> was plentiful (late summer/autumn) and then split up in winter. Such gatherings would have allowed ideas to be <u>shared</u>.

4) The infrequency of mass gatherings and the <u>lack of writing</u> would have made progress <u>slow</u>.

5) <u>Excavations</u> of ancient burials and tombs tell us about people's attitudes to <u>human remains</u> — an important factor in the advancement of <u>anatomy</u>. Some cultures <u>moved</u> the remains of the dead around and may have brought them out for <u>ceremonial purposes</u>. In some of the barrow tombs in Britain skeletons are mixed up and incomplete — skulls in one place, long bones in another etc. Other cultures probably had many more <u>taboos</u> about remains — limiting their knowledge of <u>anatomy</u>.

6) Fine and <u>delicate</u> stone tools have been found, especially flint and obsidian, which show that some <u>surgery</u> was feasible. We have evidence of trepanning, but cannot tell much about surgery on <u>soft tissues</u> due to the lack of evidence (see Archaeopathology over the page).

No soft tissues? I bet they had sore noses...

The key point about prehistory is of course that there's no writing. There's nothing to tell us what they believed — so we have to <u>deduce</u> things. And lack of writing limits the spread of knowledge — but don't forget <u>social organisation</u> and <u>education</u> are important too. Always think how factors like these relate to the history of medicine — that's what they'll ask you.

Ancient Health and Beliefs

We don't just have to rely on archaeology though — we can look at other societies too.

Ethnoarchaeology and Anthropology — going native...

Outsiders visiting prehistoric societies can produce written records of what they see — but their very contact can often change the society they look at.

1) Ancient artifacts and artwork are similar to things made by modern or more recent aboriginal societies in Australia and elsewhere. Attitudes and practices of modern aborigines have therefore been used in guessing what ancient people thought and did.

2) "Modern" aborigines combine basic practical methods like setting broken bones and bandaging with spiritual explanations of illness and cure.

3) Witch doctors and shamans are frequently credited with the ability to both cure and inflict illness. The use of the "evil eye" or "death bones" certainly worked in some cases — as does faith healing, which is still practised in industrialised societies. Modern thinkers generally attribute this to the power of suggestion.

4) Preventative medicine (warding off evil) is practised as well as healing (driving off evil). Rituals and sacrifice are often involved. Rituals might involve the use of herbs, potions and techniques of practical value — but they are seen as magic rather than medicine.

Archaeopathlogy is the study of ancient disease

1) Archaeopathology is the study of ancient bodies to see what diseases and health problems they had, how they were treated, and how the people died.

2) Most prehistoric bodies have decayed to just bones or even further. This limits the evidence that can be gained from them — e.g. you couldn't tell if someone died from a heart attack.

3) Some bodies, preserved in ice, peat bogs or by mummification, still have soft tissues remaining. They're very important for what they tell us about prehistoric health and medicine.

4) Trephining or trepanning is the cutting of holes in people's heads. Many skulls show that people survived the operation because the bone continued to grow afterwards. We cannot be certain why people did this but it may have been to allow evil spirits out or to grant special powers of communication with the spirit world.

Of course it works! No-one ever complains of a headache twice!

5) There is modern evidence that trephining can lead to altered mental sensations. It is sometimes done by doctors when head injuries lead to a build up of pressure inside the skull. Some modern people have even tried it for non-medical reasons. So ancient trephining could have been done for practical reasons — to treat injury or in an attempt to treat diseases like epilepsy.

Trepanning — a hole load of fun...

Lots more facts here. But to sum up, early societies would have had both a practical and a spiritual view of the world. It's important to realise how their thoughts would have affected their medicine. Assumptions of supernatural causes for unexplained events would have discouraged investigation or experimentation — so medical development would have been r e a l   s l o w...

SECTION ONE — PREHISTORIC MEDICINE

The Ancient Egyptian Civilisation

The Egyptians were one of the first societies to emerge from prehistory.

The society of Ancient Egypt relied on the Nile

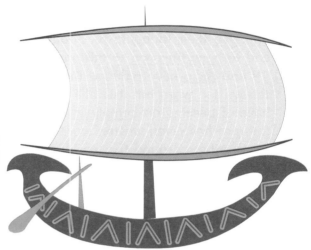

1) The Egyptian civilisation was an agricultural one that spread in a narrow band along the river Nile. It thrived between c.3400 BC and 30 BC. Every year the Nile floods fertilised the fields and the river provided water for irrigation.

2) The successful agriculture provided spare food so that more people could be doctors, priests (these two professions overlapped or were the same thing) and other professionals. The floods kept people out of the fields for part of the year, leaving large workforces free for projects like pyramid building.

3) Barges on the Nile made trade and government easier and allowed ideas to be communicated to lots of people.

The world of the Egyptians was controlled by the gods

1) The Egyptians had a huge number of Gods that controlled all aspects of life including illness and medicine. Amulets, charms and rituals were used to avoid and cure illness.

2) Sekhmet was the goddess of war who also sent and cured epidemics. Thoth was the God who gave doctors their ability to cure people. Imhotep, who was the Pharaoh Zoser's doctor in about 2630 BC, was adopted as a god of healing. Doctors were respected people.

3) Priests kept the Books of Thoth which contained the accepted treatments and spells. The books themselves have not survived but the Papyrus Ebers (so called because it was once owned by a German Egyptologist called Maurice Ebers) contains spells, potions (medicines) and procedures probably taken from the Books of Thoth.

4) Some of the drugs used by the Egyptians, including opium, are still used today. They were probably thought of as driving away evil spirits rather than affecting the way the body works.

5) The instructions are very exact as to what should be done, what medicines given and what words should be used in incantation and when talking to the patient.

6) If a doctor followed the instructions and the patient died then he was not blamed — but if he had changed the treatment or wording in any way he could be executed. This is an example of how, when medical practice becomes religious ritual, progress can be stifled.

Nile desperandum — but there's a pharaohed bit to learn...

Don't ignore all those background details at the top of the page — stuff like that helps to put it all in perspective. You need to know the factors that influenced medicine in Egypt — so that stuff's essential. The most important point here is that the Egyptians believed diseases were caused by the gods — which of course had a big say in how they were treated.

Practical Medicine in Ancient Egypt

The Egyptians had writing, which made a lot of difference to the development of their medicine.

The Secret of Immortality — Mummification or Writing?

1) By writing ideas down people have been able to preserve their thoughts for thousands of years and to pass them on to millions of other people.

2) TV and radio have reduced the importance of the written word but it is still the best way we have of passing on complicated ideas. The Internet has given written words new power to reach others around the world. Each generation reads what people in the past thought and then develops new ideas.

3) The Egyptians had writing. Their writing was made up of lots of little pictures called hieroglyphics.

They Mummified bodies, but didn't chop them up

1) The Egyptians believed that the human body would be needed by a person in the afterlife, and that material possessions would also be important. This led to their attempts (very successful) to preserve bodies and entomb them with fabulous grave goods.

2) They prepared bodies for mummification by extracting soft organs such as the brain and the intestines, then drying (desiccating) what remained with salt. This gave the Egyptians some knowledge of anatomy.

3) They believed that destroying someone's body meant they wouldn't go to the afterlife, so experimental dissection was out. This limited the amount of knowledge that could be gained.

4) The Papyrus Edwin Smith, written around 1600 BC, outlines some simple surgical procedures.

5) Carvings in the temple of Kom Ombo (c. 100 BC) show a variety of surgical instruments.

6) Willow was used after surgery and to treat wounds. It contains salicylic acid, a mild antiseptic and the original source of aspirin.

The Egyptians actually looked at their patients

1) Diagnosis merely means the observation of a patient and the recognition of their symptoms.

2) Even though it is simple in theory, diagnosis can be the most important part of the work of a doctor and can be quite tricky.

3) Egyptian writings survive that demonstrate that they included diagnosis in their medical rituals.

Mummification — the onset of parenthood...

OK, so the Egyptians had writing. That's a big point. It meant they could communicate their ideas better — and of course it's the way we know about them. Even though they thought the gods caused disease, they used their brains too. For a start, they actually looked at their patients — cunning. Make sure you know how their beliefs affected their anatomical knowledge.

Egyptian Hygiene and the Minoans

The Egyptians believed in clearing passages and cleanliness, while the Minoans went to great lengths to ensure lots of clean water.

Non-spiritual causes for illness were suggested

1) The River Nile led some Egyptians to suggest that, like the Nile delta or their irrigation systems, the body was full of channels.
2) They thought that if those channels were blocked this led to disease. This led them to use vomiting, purging (laxatives) and bleeding to clear the various passages. With the exception of bleeding, which is never good, such treatments will aid some complaints.
3) Such ideas were not accepted by everyone and the people who believed them did not abandon spiritual explanations and treatments.
4) The Egyptians knew diet was important — medical procedures included recommended foods.

The Egyptians kept themselves clean

1) The Egyptians were a clean people. They bathed, shaved their heads and had toilets. They also changed their clothes regularly.
2) In the Egyptian climate this would have made life more comfortable, but hygiene also appears to have had a religious significance. Priests washed more often than others and would shave their whole bodies before important ceremonies.
3) Egyptian toilets have been found, but they did not have water-fed sewers so the toilets had to be emptied manually.
4) Egyptians also developed mosquito nets which would have offered some protection from malaria.

The Minoans developed advanced water supply systems

1) Minoan Crete had a powerful empire from 2000 - 1380 BC.
2) The Minoans built water storage tanks and piped water around their palaces. They also had drains, sewers and toilets which were cleaned by using water to flush them out.
3) They probably used aqueducts to bring water from outside their towns.
4) The major palaces on Crete including Knossos were destroyed by fire in some catastrophe around 1380 BC. It is not clear whether this was due to a natural disaster or military invasion by the Mycenaean Greeks. The nearby island of Thera suffered a volcanic explosion at that time which could have caused earthquakes, tidal waves and showers of hot ashes on Crete.
5) The impressive features of the Minoan civilisation were lost and had to be rediscovered later. Comparable standards of plumbing did not reappear until the time of the Romans and were lost again with the fall of the Roman Empire.
6) Sir Arthur Evans found the ruins of Knossos and did a lot of excavation work around 1900.

Crete balls of fire — so that's how they died...

Right, so the Egyptians were a clean lot, which was pretty handy from the health point of view. This was partly down to luck of course — as they had little grasp of the causes of disease. A big difference between them and the Minoans was that the Minoan government played a part in improving public health — by doing a bit of high-tech plumbing. Pity they didn't fireproof it...

The Ancient Greek Civilisation

All around the Mediterranean the Greeks developed a supernatural approach to medicine.

When is a Greek not a Greek? When He's an African...

1) The notion of countries bounded by geographical borders — lines on a map — is rather recent. When we talk of the ancient Greeks we are referring, not to people who lived in Greece, but to people who lived the way the Greeks did — they were culturally Greek. Greek civilisation was made up of independent city states around the shores of the Mediterranean and the Black Sea.
2) Greek Culture flourished between 1000 BC and 300 BC and its medicine was influenced by the Egyptians.
3) Their world was controlled by many gods and they told and wrote down heroic tales (myths) about people, gods and monsters. They also loved to debate.

Greek culture involved lots of debate. Loads of views were expressed, but being in the more ardent debates could be dangerous. Socrates' enemies charged him with impiety and corrupting the young — and served him up some tasty hemlock. Two systems of medicine flourished side by side: one based on religion and one on logical philosophy.

The cult of Asclepios — faith healing

1) A spiritual/supernatural approach to medicine was followed by the cult of Asclepios, god of healing. His temples were called Asclepions and people went to stay at them when they were ill — much like we might visit a health farm or go on a pilgrimage to Lourdes. The cult was most popular in the 5th and 4th centuries BC.
2) Visitors were expected to undergo ceremonial washing in the sea, make a sacrifice to the god and sleep in a building called an abaton. An abaton was a narrow building with a roof but no solid walls so that it was open to the air. Whilst sleeping there the god was supposed to come to them in a dream and cure them. Priests also did "ward rounds", administering ointments and performing rituals, some of which involved placing snakes on the patients. The snake is the sacred animal of Asclepios and can still be seen in the logos of many medical organisations.

This is going to hurt me more than it will you

3) Success stories were recorded in inscriptions on the walls of the Asclepions.
4) Asclepios's daughters, Hygeia and Panacea, were also involved in healing. Their names developed into words used in modern medicine (hygiene — cleanliness, and panacea — a remedy for all ills). Women were allowed to be doctors in Ancient Greece.

Medicine in Grease? I bet they were smooth operators...

The key points here are that Greece was a culture rather than a country, and the Greeks believed in many gods — hence their belief in supernatural causes and cures. Remember that it's not enough to just learn these facts by rote — you've got to be prepared for the sort of things they'll ask you in the Exam. It'd really help if you could work through some past papers.

Practical Medicine in Ancient Greece

Not all Greeks left it to the gods though — they also developed a "natural" approach to medicine.

Philosophers tried to explain stuff rationally

1) Greek philosophers sought to devise rational explanations and logical codes of conduct. They attracted bands of followers such as the brotherhood of Pythagoras. These followers became devotees and argued with other philosophers. Religion was interwoven with their logic.
2) Thales of Miletus, founder of Greek philosophy, thought that water was the basis of life (c.580 BC). Anaximander (c.560 BC) said all things were made of four elements: earth, air, water and fire. Pythagoras (582?-500?BC) thought life was about the balance of opposites.

Hippocrates — the founding father of modern medicine

1) Hippocrates (460?-377?BC) is acknowledged as the founding father of modern medicine. He was born on the island of Kos, travelled a bit and then taught medicine in Kos before dying in Larissa. Very little else is known about him but he is associated with the Hippocratic Oath and the Hippocratic Corpus.
2) The Hippocratic Oath is a promise made by doctors to obey rules of behaviour in their professional lives. Medical ethics are based on the Hippocratic Oath.
3) The Hippocratic Corpus is a collection of medical books, some of which might have been written by Hippocrates or his followers. It is probably what survived of the library of the Kos school of medicine at which Hippocrates taught.

At last! A clear diagnosis — you're dead!

The ideas of the Hippocratic Corpus

1) Hippocrates saw the healthy body as being in balance — he thought that illness was an imbalance of the elements.
2) "Airs, Waters and Places" (5th century BC) looks for environmental causes for disease — not gods or spirits.
3) "Prognostic", "Coan Prognostic" and "Aphorisms" improved on the Egyptian ideas of diagnosis. They suggested that, by studying enough cases, a doctor could learn to predict the course of an illness. They also suggested that no action should be taken before a reliable diagnosis is made. Illnesses should also, where possible, be left to run their course. Today we call this "Minimum Intervention".

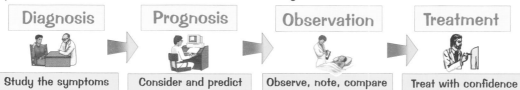

Diagnosis	Prognosis	Observation	Treatment
Study the symptoms	Consider and predict	Observe, note, compare	Treat with confidence

4) "Regimen" and "Regimen in Acute Diseases" detail suggested lifestyles for healthy living or recovery from illness. "Regimen" and "regime" are words used in English today. Ancient Greek regimens included ideas on exercise, hygiene and stress management that we would think very sensible today. The self-help guides that you can buy in bookshops are like Greek regimens.

Hippocrates — hard to spell? Think Hippo Crates

Make sure you see how Hippocrates' ideas fitted in with other Greek thought at the time. Remember that for hundreds of years his natural approach existed side by side with the supernatural ideas of the cult of Asclepios. And although the four elements theory was wrong, it was a step in the right direction.

Aristotle and Medicine in Alexandria

Aristotle developed Hippocrates' ideas, then Alexandria became a centre of medical development.

Aristotle linked disease to the four humours

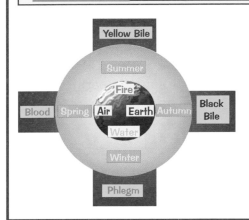

1) Aristotle (384-322BC) developed the Hippocratic balance of elements to suggest that the body was made up of four fluids or humours — blood, phlegm, yellow bile and black bile. These were linked to the four seasons and the four elements then seen as the basis of chemistry.

2) In winter we get colds and produce more phlegm. Also, it rains more. This is why Aristotle linked water, winter and phlegm. Can you see the logic in the other connections? Unfortunately, Aristotle failed to see that a bunged up nose, fevers and suchlike are symptoms or effects of disease. He thought they were the causes.

Alexandria became a centre of medical advance

1) Alexander the Great (who was tutored by Aristotle) founded Alexandria in Egypt in 332 BC as his new capital city. The library of Alexandria attempted to amass all the knowledge of the world. It made copies of books for other libraries, which was lucky as several fires eventually destroyed the collection.

Did I leave the gas on?

2) Unlike in the rest of "Greece", human dissection was allowed in Alexandria. For a short time they even allowed vivisection (dissection when still alive) of condemned criminals. People began to see the human body as having served its purpose once the soul had left it.

Bad news — you've been condemned to death. Good news — it's been reduced to community service.

3) Alexandria became famous for training medics and surgeons. Accurate observation was the key to much of the advancement made there. Herophilus (c.335-280 BC) compared human and animal anatomy and worked on the nervous system. He correctly identified the connections to the brain but thought the nerves were vessels carrying pneuma or life-force.

4) Erasistratus (c.250 BC) identified the differences between arteries, veins and nerves and saw that nerves were not hollow and so couldn't be vessels for fluid.

5) Doctors from Alexandria went to practise all over the world but also divided into competing intellectual camps which, whilst encouraging debate, also led doctors to refuse to consider anything except the teachings of their own group.

6) The mechanics of surgery advanced (which bits to cut, how to make the cut), but effective anaesthetics, antiseptics and the understanding of germs and infection were far in the future.

'Bile be black' — isn't that what Arnie said...

Just as Hippocrates had built on earlier ideas, so Aristotle built on Hippocrates' ideas. You could be asked about the development of medical ideas, so you need to think about things like that. And make sure you understand how important Alexandria was — and the two reasons why — it gathered medical knowledge together and it allowed human dissection.

Civilisation and Public Health

Greek medicine didn't disappear with the decline of Greece — it lived on in the Roman Empire.

It took a while for the Romans to accept Greek medicine

1) The Romans thought their culture was better than the then decaying Greek culture. They initially rejected the ideas of Greek medicine, which were still practised by Greeks around the Mediterranean. As the Greek cities fell to the Roman expansion many Greek doctors became slaves. Romans suspected that the Greek doctors might get revenge by poisoning them.
2) A plague in 293 BC led the Romans to establish an Asclepion in Rome, for which they brought a sacred snake from Epidaurus. This Asclepion survived throughout the Roman period and became a public hospital offering treatment to the poor and slaves.
3) Medicine and its mainly Greek practitioners slowly improved in status until Julius Caesar allowed doctors to become Roman citizens in 46 BC.

The Romans realised they needed a healthy army

1) The Romans were a very practical people. They realised that to build an empire you need a healthy army — and to make that empire pay you need a healthy population from the emperor down to the slaves.
2) So the state paid for public doctors and hospitals, starting with hospitals for wounded soldiers called "valetudinaria". Hospitals were built for more and more of the population until they had what amounted to a national health service.

They took a preventative approach to Public Health

1) The Romans' organisation, practical engineering and architecture made preventative medicine through public health measures the obvious way to progress.
2) They noticed that exposure to bad smells, unclean drinking water, sewage, swamps and dirt made you more likely to get ill, and that building temples in swamps and other supernatural means of prevention had little effect.
3) The Romans built aqueducts to carry good water into cities, public baths, toilets and sewers to remove waste. They drained swamps which were near towns. Good communication on the roads helped spread ideas. Many of the Roman structures which survive today are related to public health. How many of today's public loos do you think will still be standing in 2000 years?

Do you do it in blue?

Public Health — right up the Romans' street...

Just as the Egyptian culture didn't disappear as soon as the Greeks became more important, the Greeks didn't vanish when the Romans became the dominant culture. Think about how the two overlapping cultures led to continuity in medicine, and how the changes led to development. But just make sure you realise how important the Roman government was — what they did and why.

Dioscorides and Galen

Galen's work was influential for well over a thousand years — despite numerous inaccuracies.

Dioscorides wrote without mention of superstitions

1) Pedanius Dioscorides was a Greek doctor, born in Turkey, working for the Roman army c.AD 80.
2) His book "De Materia Medica" was the first on plants as medicines without lots of superstition.

Galen left an enduring legacy — despite many mistakes

Galen Publications
Buy My Books
They're Ace

1) Galen was a Greek born in Pergamum (a Greek city in western Turkey) in AD 129. Pergamum had become part of the Roman empire in 133 BC.
2) Pergamum had an important Asclepion at which Galen first began his training before going to Smyrna and Alexandria.
3) He returned to Pergamum where he was doctor to the gladiators and then went to Rome in AD 161.
4) He was very ambitious and worked hard at gaining a reputation. He became doctor to the Emperor's son and wrote over 100 medical texts.

Galen believed in the Humours and Observation

1) Galen supported the theories of Hippocrates on ethics and observation. He also believed in the four humours.
2) He increased his anatomical knowledge (gained from treating chopped up gladiators) by dissecting animals. He described the role of the spine in controlling the rest of the body. He couldn't dissect humans or even study a skeleton outside of Alexandria — so he resorted to chance opportunities like a rotting corpse on a gibbet, or a flash flood in a cemetery.
3) Galen was deceived by having to use only animals. He thought that the rete mirabile (a network of blood vessels on the undersurface of the brain) which he found in animals would be found in humans. It wasn't — and he described livers as the wrong shape.
4) He also let his ambition get the better of him. He only recorded his successful cases and he frequently let himself see what he wanted to see — such as tiny pores in the septum of the heart which would let blood pass from the right hand side of the heart to the left.
5) He believed that the blood started life in the liver, then passed around the body picking up various "spirits" (including "pneuma" from the lungs). It did various jobs on the way, finally being consumed rather than recirculated. He saw the nervous system as being part of this process.
6) He believed in treatment by opposites. This was based on the idea of balance of the humours.

Galen's reputation lasted some 1400 years

1) Galen had great influence on the doctors in the Arabic world and in Medieval Christian Europe.
2) His writings covered all aspects of medicine and many of the books that he wrote survived.
3) His writing was very persuasive and he did not stress the polytheistic (more than one god) side of Roman culture — so he didn't offend the later monotheistic Muslims and Christians.

A Galen of bile — that should cure 'em...

It's pretty hard to understate Galen's importance in medical history. But just stating that won't get you many marks. You need to know why he was so important. Make sure you know why his books were so influential and why he made so many mistakes — because they're the sort of things you'll be asked. So learn the facts and look at those past papers — it's the only way.

Summary for Prehistory to Classical World

OK, it's question time. They cover most of the really important points. You probably won't be able to answer a lot of them first time, but don't worry. If you can answer most of them then you're doing pretty well. Your eventual aim should be to answer all of them — and quickly. It's not hard though — it's just a matter of practice. Go through the sections and the questions enough and you'll soon be blitzing them off in no time.

1) Explain the difference between prehistory and history.
2) Which aspects of medicine are most likely to be affected by burial practices and why?
3) Name a type of surgery that we know was performed by people more than 3000 years ago.
4) How do we know that people survived this surgery?
5) What evidence do we use to suggest that spiritual cures were attempted in prehistory?
6) What geographical feature helped development and communication in the ancient Egyptian Civilisation?
7) Why were Sekhmet and Thoth important to Egyptian medicine?
8) Name the Egyptian doctor who was deified as a god of healing.
9) Suggest one reason why Egyptian doctors might have been reluctant to try out new ideas.
10) Explain how the theory and practice of mummification might have affected the development of medicine in ancient Egypt.
11) Name a painkiller and an antiseptic used in ancient Egypt.
12) What is the technical term for the observation of patients and the recognition of symptoms?
13) The geography of Egypt suggested some non-spiritual causes of illness. Explain why and describe the treatments derived from this theory.
14) What important aspect of preventative medicine was a regular part of religious ritual?
15) What did Egyptian toilets lack compared to modern ones?
16) Where was the capital of Minoan Crete?
17) Describe that aspect of the Minoan palaces which was especially important for public health.
18) Suggest two possible reasons why the Minoan's advances were lost.
19) Explain the difference between what it means to be Greek today and what it meant in the 4th Century BC.
20) Name the Greek god of healing and the temples in which the associated healing rituals were carried out.
21) What animal was sacred to the Greek god of healing? What part did it play in healing rituals?
22) How did the temples advertise their successes?
23) Describe the development of the theory of the four humours.
24) Give the approximate dates for the birth and death of Hippocrates. Explain his importance.
25) Explain the sequence of actions recommended by Hippocrates to be taken before treatment.
26) What is a regimen?
27) Where is Alexandria and when was it founded? What was its importance to ancient medicine?
28) The doctors who treated the Romans were mostly not Romans. Who were they?
29) Why was the relationship between the Romans and their doctors strained?
30) Why were the Romans prepared to invest in medicine and public health for the whole population?
31) Write a mini essay on Galen, his work and the events involving his work right up to the Rennaisance period.
32) What were Galen's major anatomical mistakes?
33) Why did Galen make the mistakes he did?

Traditional Chinese Medicine

With all these Greeks, Romans and Egyptians, it's easy to forget that there was a completely different system of medicine over in the East.

China's civilisation was old before the Egyptians

1) The Chinese first started living in farming villages about 5000 BC. By 2000 BC they had sizeable towns and writing was common.
2) Chinese medicine is based on the concept of life energies and their flow and balance.
3) Yin and Yang are the two driving forces in life that must be kept in balance. Yin is cool, passive, restful, introspective and associated with the night and shade. Yang is hot, active, outward looking and associated with the Sun and daytime. Diet and herbal or animal based medicines are used to maintain this balance along with special physical techniques.
4) Some of the medicines, especially those based on animal parts, are not highly regarded in the west but others contain valuable drugs such as the preparation of horsetail plant used for asthma that contains ephedrine. Ephedrine was "discovered" by western medicine in 1928, 1700 years after the reference to the horsetail preparation in Zhan Zhongjing's text.
5) Inoculation against smallpox originated in China before spreading West via Turkey.

If life's needling you try acupuncture

1) Life energy is called qi (chi). Chinese medicine states that this qi flows around the body in invisible channels.
2) Illness disrupts and blocks the flow of qi and inserting fine needles is thought to re-establish the correct flow and balance of yin and yang. Complex charts and even models show practitioners where to insert needles to relieve pain in different parts of the body. The right points have to be stimulated to gain the desired pain relief.
3) Acupuncture certainly works as pain relief. It is used more and more alongside western medicine as a complimentary technique and can even be used as an anaesthetic for surgery in people who cannot or will not use anaesthetic drugs.

Could moxibustion light your fire?

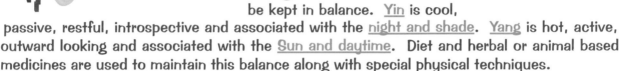

1) Moxibustion is the burning of small cones of mugwort (a herb) close to the relevant acupuncture points.
2) It is supposed to warm the qi, assisting flow.

Hmm — I wonder if they used qi hole surgery...

The thing about Chinese medicine is that it developed in isolation — and it followed a very different path from much of western medicine. Writing also played a big part in its development, just like in Egypt. Unlike the Egyptians though, gods played little if any role. They did have some similar ideas though — like that of channels in the body. Now learn those picky details.

Traditional Indian Medicine

And it wasn't just China — India had two traditions of medicine too.

Ayurveda and Unani — two forms of Indian medicine

1) The Ayurveda medicine is as old as Chinese medicine, whilst Unani medicine is based on Greek ideas including the four humours/elements.
2) Ayurveda drugs are herb, animal and mineral based.
3) Doctors underwent training at two major schools — at Taxila and Barnaras.
4) Most treatment was done at home, but after 274 BC there were hospitals for the very sick.

We know their ideas from their medical books

1) Susruta, who taught surgery at Barnaras in the 4th century AD, wrote a book called Susruta Samhita. It travelled west on the Silk Road and was translated into Arabic in the AD 700s.
2) The anatomy in this book is not of a very accurate standard but the surgery described included operations on eyes, ears, and noses, the setting of fractures and Caesarean births. In addition the use of cannabis and henbane as anaesthetics is described. The symptoms of various important diseases are given
3) The most important surviving traditional Indian medical text is the Charaka Samhita. It was written by Chakrapanditta in AD 1066.

Traditional medicine is still taught in India

1) Both Ayurveda medicine and Unani medicine are still taught in some 108 institutions in India, including the Ayurveda University at Jamnagar.

The Mongol Empire fostered world trade

1) During the 13th century AD the Mongol Empire spread to include both India and China. Kublai Kahn moved his capital to what is now Beijing and founded the Yuan dynasty.
2) Although ruthless in the extreme, their empire encouraged trade and the exchange of ideas — both practical and religious. Muslim traders brought medicines from Persia and elsewhere into the empire overland by camel trains and Christian traders began to reach the shores of China by ship.
3) Europeans also improved communication with the East as they searched for the mythical Prester John, an Eastern Christian King who would save them from the Mongols.

Yuan't going to believe this — it Khan't be true...

When you think of eastern medicine, you tend to think of the Chinese. It's easy to forget that India has its own medical tradition. The Mongol Empire certainly had an effect on Chinese and Indian medicine, but maybe not such a catastrophic effect as you'd have thought — it allowed the communication of ideas — essential for the development of medicine. Learn and enjoy...

Imperial Collapse and the Dark Ages

The Roman Empire didn't last forever. It weakened, split, then fell. That wasn't good for medicine.

The collapse of the Roman Empire led to the Dark Ages

1) The Roman Empire split into an Eastern Empire and a Western Empire in AD 395. In AD 410 the Goths invaded Italy and Roman troops were withdrawn from provinces, including Britain.

2) The last Roman Emperor in the West was deposed by a German Chieftain in AD 476. This led to a very rapid collapse of social organisation, technical skills and academic knowledge.

3) In AD 431 Nestorius, the Christian Patriarch of Jerusalem, was banished for heresy and travelled further East to Persia. There he set up a centre of medical learning that translated the works of Hippocrates and Galen into Arabic.

4) The knowledge of the Greek and Roman eras migrated east and was lost, but not irretrievably, from the western end of the Mediterranean and Europe.

Barbarians and superstition swept across Europe

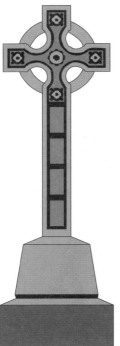

1) In Britain the partly Romanised and partly Christian Celts were gradually overwhelmed by waves of pagan Saxons coming across the North Sea. They brought with them a return to medical cures based mostly on superstition and magic. So complete was the loss of knowledge that by AD 700 the Saxons believed that the ruins of Roman architecture they saw around them were the work of giants and other mythical beings.

2) Not only did the public health systems of the Romans fall into disrepair, but the people of the Dark Ages lacked the education to understand the value of hygiene, clean water etc. Many of the Roman towns were abandoned in favour of small dispersed farmsteads.

3) The Christian Church re-established itself in Britain from both the east and the west — St. Augustine arrived in Kent in AD 597, and Celtic monks came from Ireland. The Synod of Whitby (AD 663) brought about the dominance of the Roman version of Christianity — and brought Britain into the church that would maintain a mere shadow of the communication and unity that had been seen in the western Roman Empire.

The Dark Ages — a black time for medicine...

The fall of the Roman Empire really did have a devastating effect on medicine. This was one of the biggest turning points in the history of medicine — one of those things Examiners love to ask you about. Make sure you understand the factors involved in the loss of knowledge — like the superstitious and magical beliefs of the Saxons, and the role of government.

The Arab World

All was not lost though — many Greek medical texts were preserved by the Arabic empire.

Arab doctors maintained and improved on the Classics

1) Aristotle's four humours, Galen's treatment by opposites and Hippocrates' clinical observation lived on with the Arabists (the name given to those following Arabic schools of medicine).

2) In the ninth century, Hunain ibn Ishaq (a.k.a. Johannitius) travelled from Baghdad, the capital of the new Islamic Arab empire, to Greece to collect medical texts. He translated these into Arabic.

3) In about AD 910 al-Razi (or Rhazes) distinguished smallpox and measles as separate diseases.

4) Avicenna, a Persian (AD 980 - 1037), wrote the "Canon of Medicine" which brought together the ideas of Aristotle, Galen and Hippocrates. This book was the most important means by which the classical ideas got back into Western Europe.

5) In the 12th century Avenzoar described the parasite that causes scabies and began to question the infallibility of Galen — as did Ibn al-Nafis in the 13th century, who suggested (correctly) that the blood flowed from one side of the heart to the other via the lungs — and did not cross the septum. Ibn al-Nafis' work was unknown in the West until the 20th century.

6) Despite Islamic prohibition on human dissection some progress in surgery was made and Albucasis (born c.AD 936) wrote a well thought out book describing amputations, the removal of bladder stones and dental surgery — as well as methods for handling fractures and dislocations and the sewing of wounds.

7) Women doctors were allowed in the Arab world at around this time.

Public health and social organisation were better too

1) The Arabic empire maintained medical schools and doctors took examinations from AD 931.

2) Major cities such as Baghdad, Cairo, Damascus and Cordoba had piped water, public baths and hospitals before the beginning of the second millennium.

Blood crossing the heart — how Nafis that?...

Right, so it was the Arabic empire to the rescue. But they didn't just translate texts — they made some progress, even if hindered like many Greeks and Romans by religious objections to human dissection. Make sure you understand the importance of the Islamic governments — especially their introduction of medical schools and exams — and the effect these had.

The Arab World

The Arabs didn't just preserve medical learning — they liked to dabble in a bit of <u>alchemy</u> too.

The <u>Arabists</u> were keen on <u>Chemistry</u>

1) <u>Alchemy</u> traces its origins back to the <u>Egyptians</u> and, like much else of ancient and classical learning, it was preserved by the <u>Arabic</u> empire. Alchemy sought to find ways of turning <u>base</u> (ordinary) metals into <u>gold</u> and to discover the elixir of <u>eternal life</u>.

Unlike modern chemistry, much <u>superstition</u> was included — an unsuccessful experiment was as likely to be blamed on the position of the <u>stars</u> or the spiritual purity of the <u>alchemist</u> as anything else.

2) Even so Arabic alchemists invented useful <u>techniques</u> such as distillation and sublimation, and prepared useful <u>drugs</u> such as laudanum, benzoin and camphor.

Not everyone in the <u>Islamic world</u> approved

1) <u>Avicenna's</u> interest in the <u>Greek Philosophers</u> produced enemies such as <u>al-Ghazali</u> who wrote "<u>Destruction of the Philosophers</u>" and encouraged a decline in rationalist philosophy in the Islamic world.

2) Avicenna did not believe in <u>personal immortality</u>, or that God was interested in <u>individuals</u>. He did not believe the <u>world creation</u> story either. This goes against the <u>orthodox</u> Islamic tradition. Even so, Avicenna was one of Islam's most influential philosophers.

3) The rise to power of the <u>Mamelukes</u> (slave-soldiers) in <u>1250</u> brought a new hardness to the Islamic world. This was partly in response to the excesses of the <u>Christian crusades</u>.

Alchemists and Apothecaries had a lot of pots to carry...

Don't ignore alchemy — the search for an <u>elixir</u> of life says a lot about medical knowledge of the time, and of course many useful <u>techniques</u> and <u>drugs</u> were developed. And don't forget — always try to relate what you read to the <u>themes</u> and <u>factors</u> from Section 1. If you can't remember them, then it's probably about time you <u>reread</u> the section. So read and enjoy...

SECTION SIX — MEDIEVAL MEDICINE

Medieval Europe Emerges

Over the centuries, the old Greek and Roman learning gradually made their way back to the West.

Galen returns to Western Europe

1) By about 1100 versions of the works of Galen and Hippocrates were coming back into Western Europe bit by bit. Arabic texts based on them, especially Avicenna's Canon, were being translated into Latin in Spain (which was partly Christian and partly Islamic) and Italy. The crusades had also made Europeans aware of the scientific knowledge of the Arabists.

2) About the same time medical schools began to appear in Western Europe, starting with the one in Salerno, Italy. This taught both men and women and had some women professors. Translations of the Arabic versions of Galen and Hippocrates were accepted as absolute truth.

3) Clinical observation and the four humours were taught. There was some realisation of the importance of cleanliness. Cistercian monks washed their feet once a week and bathed four times a year.

4) More and more schools sprang up (Montpellier, Bologna, Padua, Paris) and human dissection gained acceptance. Debates and new research led to some doubts about the classical texts.

5) Some new techniques were developed including diagnosis by urine samples. Colour and taste were used. This is a good aid to diagnosis, which is why doctors still ask for urine samples from patients today — although modern doctors don't have to rely on taste for analysis!

6) Doctors also believed that the stars caused disease and relied heavily on astrology in making diagnoses and deciding on treatments.

7) In tenth century England there was a Law of Edgar which allowed women to train as doctors.

8) As medicine re-emerged as a specialised and high status profession with guilds, it became a male preserve. The Guild of Surgeons got the Law of Edgar revoked in the fifteenth century.

Trained doctors weren't the only healers

1) Trained doctors were very expensive. Much of the medicine practised amongst the ordinary people was provided by the monasteries, apothecaries and housewife-physicians, using traditional cures and experience as their main tools.

2) The Church had access to the Latin texts used by doctors. Religious orders, especially the Hospitalers, were devoted to healing. The Church set up some public hospitals, both general and specialised (e.g. maternity hospitals and leper hospitals) — but there were never enough.

3) Apothecaries sold drugs and medicine — and sometimes advised on their use. The influence of wise-women herbalists on the apothecaries led the Apothecaries' Guild to admit women. This ancient connection was used much later by Elizabeth Garrett Anderson to allow women back into medicine.

4) The term housewife-physician covers quite a range of people from "wise women" to the lady of the manor, who was often expected to provide medical help and advice to those families on her husband's lands.

Skeerg! — the return of the Greeks...

You haven't heard the last of those Greeks. It's hard to understate the influence they had in Medieval Europe — but it wasn't all good. There's few better ways to stifle progress than accepting something as the absolute truth. Make sure you know the other factors that held things back — like the religious and social attitudes to surgery and human dissection.

European Surgery and Public Health

Medieval surgery was not the respected profession that it is today. Little progress was made.

Anatomy and Surgery — messy work for menials

You just can't get the staff these days!

Liver Mathther?

1) Unlike today when surgeons are the most respected doctors, medieval surgery was held in such low regard that it was often left to low paid assistants and untrained barber-surgeons (i.e. the local barber).

2) The dissection of corpses as teaching aids began in about 1300 and slowly brought standards of anatomy back to Roman levels and beyond — but progress was slow as the assistants who carried out dissections were required to find what the books and their betters told them to, rather than anything new or different.

3) Surgical treatments were still few and simple, as pain, bleeding and infection made major surgery very risky.

4) Attempts were made at both antiseptics and anaesthetics, but they were not widely adopted. As no notion of infection by germs existed the use of wine as a mild antiseptic by Hugh of Lucca and his son Theoderic in the early 13th century was prompted by empirical observation (they just noticed that it worked). A recipe for an anaesthetic by John of Arderne in 1376 included hemlock, opium and henbane (a relative of deadly nightshade). In carefully controlled doses this may have worked — but was very likely to kill.

Public health measures were almost non-existent

Water — never touch it. Unholy stuff!

1) As towns and cities began to reappear there was none of the central organisation or willingness by the wealthy to provide water and sewerage — like that seen in the time of the Romans.

2) Only really the monasteries made much effort to provide clean running water and effective toilets. Even the wealthy in the towns had to rely on inadequate cesspits and adjacent wells — or water courses that were little more than open sewers. Those without a cesspit frequently disposed of waste into the street in the hope that it would wash away.

3) It is little wonder that people found it healthier to drink wine and beer or buy water brought in on pack animals from outside the towns. Most wealthy houses and monasteries brewed their own beer — providing large quantities of low alcohol "small beer" for servants. The brewing process involves boiling, which sterilises the beer.

4) Some town corporations (councils) tried to regulate against the most gross practices. Without real understanding of the risks there was little will and less financial support to do anything effective. Plagues and epidemics led to some efforts being made, but usually too late.

The Middle Ages — beer today, bone tomorrow...

Medieval doctors and surgeons might have followed Greek and Roman practice — but alas, the same wasn't true of their governments. Medieval towns were filthy — but in most cases nothing was done. Make sure you understand why. Try comparing Medieval Europe with the Roman Empire, and try to explain the similarities and differences — it's excellent Exam practice.

The Black Death

Medieval conditions were a tad <u>unwholesome</u>. It was only a matter of time before disaster struck.

Armageddon in the 14th century — the Black Death

1) The <u>Black Death</u> was a series of <u>plagues</u> that first swept Europe in the mid <u>14th century</u>. Two illnesses were involved: <u>pneumonic plague</u>, spread by coughs and sneezes (airborne), and <u>bubonic plague</u>, spread by black rat flea bites. <u>Black rats</u> were carried overseas by <u>ships</u>.

2) Black Death arrived in <u>Britain</u> in <u>1348</u>. Its victims were struck down suddenly and mostly died. Between a <u>third</u> and a <u>half</u> of the population were killed. From <u>1347-1351</u>, <u>75 million</u> people died from it worldwide. Later outbreaks included the <u>Great Plague of London</u> in <u>1665</u>.

No Good?

ℕ𝕆 𝔾𝕆𝕆𝔻!

3) This devastation affected the <u>labour market</u> and patterns of land ownership. It affected the ability of the country to raise armies. It changed use of farm land. It was partly responsible for the <u>abandonment</u> of many villages.

4) People thought it was a <u>judgement from God</u>, or caused by the <u>planets</u>. They thought it was caused by <u>foul air</u>, or looked for some group of people to blame such as the <u>Jews</u> or the <u>nobility</u>.

5) Many thought the <u>end of the world</u> was near and looked for signs of <u>Armageddon</u>. Some people tried to appease the <u>Wrath of God</u> by becoming <u>flagellants</u>, whipping themselves and praying.

6) It took a very <u>brave</u> person to help someone with the disease. So afraid were some people that they <u>burnt</u> suspected plague bearers <u>alive</u>. Some doctors and clergymen did try to help and took all the <u>precautions</u> they could think of. Strong smelling <u>posies</u> were used to counter the <u>foul airs</u> believed to carry the disease. All-over <u>suits</u> were worn which might have filtered out airborne germs and provided a temporary barrier against fleas. Ships were made to wait <u>40 days</u> before landing — the word "<u>quarantine</u>" comes from the French "<u>quarante</u>", meaning 40.

Ring a ring of roses,	— Buboes (swollen lymph glands)
A pocket full of posies,	— Flowers and scents for foul airs
Atishoo, atishoo,	— Feverish symptoms
We all fall down.	— Rapidly followed by **DEATH**

I'M BACK!

7) How would you feel if it happened to <u>us</u>? <u>AIDS</u>, <u>BSE</u>, <u>E-coli</u> and <u>meningitis</u> have been in the news and have <u>worried</u> lots of people when relatively <u>small numbers</u> have died. What would it be like if <u>one third</u> of your classmates suddenly died? If you really want <u>nightmares</u> consider the fact that <u>mutating viruses</u> could produce an <u>epidemic</u> just as bad as the <u>Black Death</u> — and we have <u>no cure</u> for viruses.

Don't plague aims — this black death is serious stuff...

Not much fun this page, I'm afraid — but that doesn't mean you can ignore it. The essential point is that Medieval Europe was faced with something it <u>didn't understand</u> — and something it was <u>helpless</u> to prevent. And since they didn't have an understanding of the <u>cause</u>, not many lessons were learned — so it's no surprise the plague <u>returned</u> later.

Renaissance and Reformation

A return to classical ideas and the reformation of the church — turning points for medicine.

Renaissance Man — born-again Roman?

Leonardo da Vinci

1) The Renaissance gets its name from the rebirth of interest in the ideas of the classical period.

2) The Renaissance saw the emergence of science as we know it today from the magic and mysticism of the medieval alchemists and astrologers. The Royal Society, Britain's most prestigious scientific body, was founded in 1660. Science began to oust superstition, astrology and religion from medicine.

3) Renaissance Man is a very important concept. Academics during the Renaissance thought that a well educated person should be proficient in science and art. We remember people like Leonardo da Vinci and Michelangelo separately for their artistry and their science — but they would not have seen any clear division. Great artists therefore attended dissections of human corpses and wrote on scientific subjects using wonderful illustrations.

4) The return of the works of the great classical authors such as Hippocrates and Galen via the Arabic translations led to renewed faith in the four humours, treatment by opposites, including bleeding, and various herbal remedies.

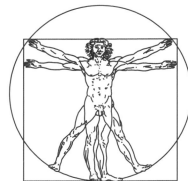

The Reformation bred new ideas

1) Attempts to take religious thought and practice back to the classical times of the early church led many to break away from the Roman Catholic church, which had dominated European religion since paganism and the elimination of the Celtic Christians. Different groups went different ways — encouraging debate and the questioning of accepted ideas.

2) Such changes were bound to produce reactionaries who were a threat to the thinkers of the Renaissance. Galileo Galilei was persecuted by the Inquisition in 1633.

Come in and talk about Science. BYO kindling.

3) Even so Paracelsus began his lecturing career in Basel in 1527 by burning one of Galen's books and calling him a liar and Avicenna a kitchen master. More importantly he rejected the idea of the four humours. He gave his lectures in German instead of the academic language of Latin, and opened them to anyone who wanted to attend — including barber-surgeons.

Paracelsus? I prefer aspirin myself...

Lots of background stuff here — but you do need to know it. The Renaissance and Reformation were major turning points for medicine — but make sure you know why. As always, think of the factors in Section 1, and think which ones were involved. That'll help you tie things together, and remember them. Whatever you do, don't get those "Re" words confused.

Public Health, War and the Plague of London

Factorising — it ain't just for mathematicians. War, communication, chance, religion, science and government action are all here. No special people for a change.

Public Health was made worse by War

1) Public health had not improved much since the medieval period.

2) The Renaissance was a very violent period. Religious differences led to many wars. Larger mercenary armies fought long inconclusive conflicts, such as the Italian Wars and the Thirty Years' War (1618-1648).

3) Populations were beginning to rise in the towns and cities, placing more strain on the available clean water supplies and sewage disposal systems.

4) People tried to build new houses within town defences. Suburbs outside town walls were often burnt down when war threatened. These were often owned by the poorest people.

5) Warfare gobbled up resources, destroyed crops and bottled people up in besieged towns without enough food. Starvation, camp fever (Typhoid), plague and sexually transmitted diseases followed the armies around the continent, killing far more than muskets or cannon.

6) Homelessness and those crippled by war put unsustainable pressures on parish structures intended for poor relief.

7) Naval power and the science of navigation improved worldwide communication. Here is one of the few examples of communication as a negative factor. Diseases common in Europe like smallpox, measles and syphilis were communicated to the new worlds, while cholera was on its way to Europe from the East. Tobacco also came back from America to blight public health for centuries to come.

The Great Plague of London 1665

DEAD!
I said, "Bring out your DEAD!"

1) This was the worst of the not infrequent reappearances of the Black Death.

2) The death toll in London was about 100,000 and many fled from the city.

3) Some efforts were made to control the spread of the disease. Afflicted households locked themselves in and painted their door with a red cross and the words, "Lord have mercy upon us." Carts organised by the authorities roamed the city to the now infamous cry of "Bring out your dead!" collecting corpses for mass burial in "plague pits".

4) Such measures showed that people realised that the disease was contagious, but they still didn't understand about germs.

5) Doctors, chemists and priests were worse affected than average because it was to them that the sick went for help.

6) The Great Fire of London in 1666 effectively sterilised large parts of London, killing the plague bacteria.

War, Famine, Pestilence and DEATH — the Fab Four...

What joy, what fun. More gory bits to learn. Remember to learn about new problems and regressions as well as the cures and developments. If you want the right atmosphere for this page go and watch "The Last Valley" with Omar Sharif and Michael Caine (as the only Cockney-German Mercenary in the Thirty Years' War.) Now scribble down those facts and enjoy...

Printing and Anatomy Books

Pressed for time? Don't ignore this page — it's important...

Printing — one of the greatest inventions of all time

1) Johann Gutenberg introduced printing to Europe in 1454. This invention accelerated the rate of progress in medicine and everything else. William Caxton set up the first British printing press in 1476 in Westminster Abbey.

2) Making a single copy of a book by hand could take many months or even years for a copyist. Books were therefore very rare and precious before printing. New ideas would have to be thoroughly accepted before anyone would go to the bother of copying them. How could ideas gain acceptance or be debated widely if they were never available as books?

3) Between 1500 and 1531 more complete copies of Galen's works, especially "On the Use of Parts" and "On Anatomical Procedures" came out of the East, were translated into Latin and published by use of the printing press. The most common version of Galen used before that was Mondino de Luzzi's book "Anatomy" of 1316, based on fragments of "On the Use of Parts".

Vesalius wrote anatomy books with accurate diagrams

Some people will steal anything!

1) Vesalius was born in 1514 and studied anatomy in Louvain and Paris. He was allowed to perform dissections, but not to boil up bodies to get skeletons. He pinched a rather ripe body from a gibbet — dirty job, but someone's got to do it.

2) After an argument in Louvain over bleeding techniques he became professor of surgery and anatomy at Padua.

3) He did his own dissections rather than employing a menial demonstrator, and he wrote books based on his observations using accurate diagrams to illustrate his work. The most important were "Tablulae Sex" ("six pictures", 1538) and "The Fabric of the Human Body" (1543).

4) His illustrations were carefully annotated so that he could refer to specific parts in the text. He oversaw all stages in the production so that it was all as he wanted it. His work served to point out some of Galen's mistakes: In the second edition of "The Fabric" Vesalius said there were no holes in the septum of the heart — and his successor, Columbo, said (1559) that blood went from one side of the heart to the other via the lungs. This was 300 years after Ibn al-Nafis.

I'm bleeding right!

No you're bleeding not!

Hey PRESSto — surgery by the book...

Communication is of course one of the key factors you might be asked about — and for good reason. Remember that lack of communication was probably the biggest factor hindering the development of medicine through the Middle Ages. The printing press changed all that. Think how much harder it would have been for Vesalius to make a difference without it.

Paré and Harvey

Bored? Harvey look at this...

Paré _was forced to improvise — and improved as well_

1) Ambroise Paré was a barber-surgeon born in 1510. Surgery was still a low status profession. Paré worked for a public hospital, then became an army surgeon.

2) At the time the severed blood vessels left by amputation were sealed by burning their ends using a red hot iron (cautery). This caused extreme discomfort for the already stressed patient. Paré invented the method of tying off vessels with threads (ligatures). He also designed quite sophisticated artificial legs.

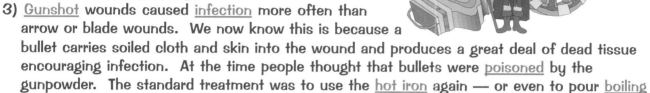

War is Hell! The red hot iron, the boiling oil — and that's just what we do to our own side!

3) Gunshot wounds caused infection more often than arrow or blade wounds. We now know this is because a bullet carries soiled cloth and skin into the wound and produces a great deal of dead tissue encouraging infection. At the time people thought that bullets were poisoned by the gunpowder. The standard treatment was to use the hot iron again — or even to pour boiling oil into the wound. This may have worked in some cases, but would have caused more harm than good.

Ambroise Paré

4) During one battle Paré ran out of oil and resorted to a simple cool salve instead. To his surprise the patients treated that way did better than the ones scalded with the oil.

5) Eventually he became surgeon to the King of France, but his ideas were resisted by doctors who thought that a lowly surgeon should not be listened to. It took the King's support to gain him acceptance.

Harvey discovered the circulation of the blood

1) William Harvey was born in 1578 and studied medicine and anatomy at Padua. He then worked in London as a doctor and a lecturer at the Royal College of Surgeons, before becoming Royal Physician to James I and Charles I.

2) He did comparative studies (c.1615) on animals and humans. He realised that he could observe living animal hearts in action and his findings would also apply to humans.

3) Galen had thought that the blood was formed, carried to the tissues and then consumed. Harvey realised this was wrong. His logic for suggesting circulation was that too much blood was being pumped out of the heart for it to be continually formed and consumed — so it must be going round and round. He also identified the difference between arteries and veins, which built on the discoveries of Erasistratus (c.250 BC) — and he noticed that blood changes colour as it passes through the lungs.

4) Although a very important discovery and a turning point in anatomy, Harvey's work did not radically change the practice of surgery. Bleeding continued to be performed and blood transfusions were not generally successful until the discovery of blood groups in 1900.

Oil be darned — this could salve a few lives...

Two key developments here, both due to the brilliance of individuals. Harvey and other doctors could only observe dead human hearts — for obvious reasons — so the heart was badly understood. It took Harvey's cunning to get round the problem. Don't forget that Paré needed the King's help to get his message across — a good example of the effect of social attitudes.

Summary for Eastern to Renaissance

That's another big chunk covered so it's time for more fiendish questions. Some of these are fairly straightforward tests of what you know. Others test your ability to use the facts you've learnt to make an argument — Remember the stuff in the Introduction: Recall, Select, Organise, Deploy.

1) The basis of Eastern medicine is life energies and their flow and balance. Discuss this and the differences between the Eastern and Western approaches.
2) Name one Eastern drug that is respected in the West, and one that is not.
3) Where did inoculation originate and how did it reach Britain?
4) Explain the theories and practice of acupuncture and moxibustion.
5) Name the two forms of Indian medicine and explain the difference between them.
6) Discuss the effects of the Mongol Empire on the development of world medicine.
7) When was the last western Roman emperor deposed and by whom?
8) Nestorius was important in protecting medical knowledge. Who was he and what did he do?
9) Where was the meeting that brought Britain into the Roman Catholic Church?
10) Discuss the effect of the Roman Catholic Church on medicine in the medieval period.
11) Names you are not used to can be hard to remember. Explain the work of the Arabists associated with: a) the collection and translation of Greek texts   b) smallpox
                 c) the "Canon of Medicine"   d) scabies   e) the cardiovascular system.
12) Describe the developments made in public health and medical training in Arabic cities by AD 1000.
13) What was the primary aim of the alchemists? What did they actually achieve?
14) Why did Avicenna's work provoke hostility amongst some scholars of the time?
15) Name a book that was important in bringing the ideas of Hippocrates and Galen back into Western Europe. How did it get to the West?
16) What was the general attitude towards the writings of the classical scholars in Medieval Europe? How did this affect the rate of change?
17) What did one of the Laws of King Edgar allow women to do? When did this change and why?
18) Were University-trained doctors the most common medical practitioners available to the people of Medieval Britain? What alternatives were there?
19) Who usually carried out anatomical dissection and surgery? Were they respected people?
20) Compare government and social attitudes to public health in medieval Britain and in the Roman Empire. Discuss their effects.
21) Outline an empirical attempt at antisepsis made in the early 13th century. Why is it described as empirical?
22) When and how did the Black Death reach Europe and what proportion of the population died?
23) What causes were suggested for the Black Death?
24) What practical and spiritual measures did people take in response to the Black Death?
25) Name a "Renaissance Man" interested in human dissections.
26) Explain the term "Renaissance Man" as it is applied beyond the meaning of a man who lived in Renaissance times.
27) Name the important scientific institution founded in 1660.
28) How did Paracelsus accelerate the rate of change in medical theory?
29) What invention allowed Vesalius to make his important contribution? How did he use it to best advantage?
30) War and chance were important in Paré's achievements, but so was personal determination. Explain the effects of these factors in his story.
31) Discuss Harvey's work on the circulation of the blood. Was it a turning point in anatomy, surgery or both? Use your knowledge to support your opinion.

The Age of Enlightenment

Jenner's <u>vaccination</u> was a landmark in the development of <u>preventative medicine</u>.

Lady Montagu introduced Inoculation from Turkey

1) Plague was less of a killer in the <u>18th century</u> than <u>smallpox</u>. This terrible disease was frequently <u>fatal</u> and left the lucky survivors badly <u>scarred</u> and <u>disfigured</u>.
2) <u>Lady Mary Wortley Montagu</u> learnt about <u>inoculation</u> in <u>Turkey</u> and introduced it to Britain. Inoculation had arrived in Turkey from <u>China</u>.
3) There were <u>mild forms</u> of the disease and a thread <u>soaked in pus</u> from a sore of someone with mild smallpox could be used to <u>immunise</u> other healthy people. The thread was drawn through a <u>small cut</u> in the person to be inoculated. After a mild reaction they were immune to smallpox.
4) Unfortunately inoculation sometimes led to <u>full-blown</u> smallpox and death. The fear of smallpox led people to take the <u>risk</u> of inoculation. Doctors could become <u>rich</u> doing inoculations.

Jenner was very interested in Milkmaids

1) <u>Edward Jenner</u> (b. <u>1749</u>) was a country doctor in <u>Gloucestershire</u>. He heard that <u>milkmaids</u> didn't get smallpox, but they did catch the much milder <u>cowpox</u>.
2) Using careful <u>scientific methods</u> Jenner investigated and discovered that it was true that people who had had <u>cowpox</u> didn't get <u>smallpox</u>.
3) In <u>1796</u> Jenner was ready to <u>test</u> his theory. He took a small boy called <u>James Phipps</u> and injected him with <u>pus</u> from the sores of <u>Sarah Nelmes</u>, a milkmaid with <u>cowpox</u>. Jenner then injected him with <u>smallpox</u>. James didn't catch the disease.
4) The Latin for cow, <u>vacca</u>, gives us the word <u>vaccination</u>.

Jenner became world famous, but not everyone was happy

1) <u>Smallpox</u> was taken to <u>America</u> by the white Europeans, and Jenner's <u>vaccinations</u> made him famous even amongst the <u>Native Americans</u>, who sent a delegation to England to thank him.
2) In <u>1802</u> and <u>1806</u> Parliament gave Jenner <u>£10,000</u> and <u>£20,000</u> respectively — equivalent to <u>millions</u> today. In <u>1840</u> vaccination was made <u>free</u> for infants — and <u>compulsory</u> in <u>1853</u>.
3) Some people were opposed to vaccination. Doctors performing <u>inoculation</u> saw it as a threat to their livelihood and many people were worried about giving themselves a disease from <u>cows</u>.

Boerhaave and Hunter — advanced diagnosis and surgery

1) <u>Herman Boerhaave</u> taught Medicine at Leyden between <u>1718</u> and <u>1729</u>. His major contribution was to suggest the use of detailed <u>case notes</u> and <u>post-mortems</u> for better diagnoses.
2) Because he was a teacher his ideas <u>spread quickly</u> as his students moved away to work.
3) <u>John Hunter</u> started working as a surgeon in London in <u>1763</u> and became Surgeon General to the Army and Surgeon Extraordinary to the <u>King</u>.
4) His success was due to his <u>skill</u> and his <u>innovations</u>. He invented the <u>tracheotomy</u> (a cut in the trachea to bypass a blocked windpipe).

Inoculation, vaccination — it's all immunisation to me...

People afraid of giving themselves a disease from cows — let me BSE, where have I heard that before? Vaccination is a brilliant example of <u>government action</u> to improve public health. Don't forget that the <u>causes</u> of disease weren't understood, so how vaccination worked was a mystery. It's development was solely based on Jenner's <u>observation</u> and <u>clear thinking</u>.

Developments in Nursing

Horrific conditions during the Crimean War brought two nurses to the public's attention.

The "Lady with the Lamp" changed nursing

F. Nightingale

1) Florence Nightingale brought a new sense of discipline and professionalism to a job that had a very bad reputation at the time.
2) She became a nurse despite the opposition of her family, and studied in Europe from 1849 and in Alexandria in 1850.
3) In 1853 she was appointed the Superintendent at the Institution for the Care of Sick Gentlewomen. At this stage she was already interested in the training of nurses.
4) The Crimean War broke out in March 1854. The use of telegraphic communications by war correspondents to get stories home fast encouraged people to have opinions and comment.
5) Horror stories emerged about the Barrack Hospital in Scutari, where the British wounded were being treated.
6) Sidney Herbert, who was both the Secretary of War and a friend of the Nightingale family, requested that Florence went to Scutari to sort out the nursing care in the hospital. Despite opposition from the military, Florence took 38 hand-picked nurses in the Autumn of 1854 and created a legend to rival the Charge of the Light Brigade. More reliable evidence of her success was the death rate in the hospital — 42% before she arrived, but 2% in 1856.

Mother Seacole also nursed in the Crimea

1) Mary Jane Seacole fits the stereotype of the medieval "wise woman".
2) She learnt nursing from her mother, who ran a boarding house for invalid soldiers in Kingstown, Jamaica, and came to England to volunteer for the Crimea.
3) She was rejected, possibly on racist grounds, but went anyway, paying her own passage.
4) Financing herself by selling medicines to the soldiers, she nursed soldiers on the battlefields.
5) She couldn't find work as a nurse in England after the war and went bankrupt — though she did receive support due to the press interest in her story. She wrote an autobiography.

Florence Nightingale returned with a mission

1) Florence Nightingale used her fame to help her change the face of nursing forever.
2) Her book, "Notes on Nursing", explained her methods — the standard textbook for generations.
3) £44,000 was raised to help her train nurses, and she set up the Nightingale School of Nursing in St. Thomas's Hospital, London. Discipline and attention to detail were important.
4) She wanted nurses to remain single so that they wouldn't have divided loyalties. She'd turned down offers of marriage when she wanted to start her career in 1844. Of the 38 nurses she took to the Crimea, 24 were nuns. Although partly due to the poor standard of training outside the convents, this also suggests that she thought of nursing like a religious vocation.
5) The 1919 Registration of Nurses Act made training compulsory for nurses.
6) It wasn't until 1960 that men were admitted to the Royal College of Nurses.

Like it or lamp it, you've got to learn it...

When you think of turning points, it's so easy to just think of watershed discoveries — and forget about things like nursing, which have often made just as much difference. Make sure you know exactly what both the nurses did — and why Florence Nightingale had much more influence. Also think back to the factors on page 3 — they're nearly all involved here.

Germs and the Fight Against Them

Slightly later, in France, Pasteur had the germ of an idea.

The Uphill Struggle
against Germs

1941 Florey — mass-produced penicillin
1932 Domagk — sulphonamides
1928 Fleming — discovers penicillin
1911 Ehrlich — develops Salvarsan 606
1891 von Behring — develops diptheria antitoxin
1884 Metchnikoff — discovers phagocytes
1882 Koch — identifies TB microbe
1857 Pasteur — Germ Theory

Pasteur was the first to suggest that germs cause disease

L. Pasteur

1) Micro-organisms had been seen through 18th century microscopes, but scientists thought they were caused by disease and appeared because of illness. This was the theory of spontaneous generation. Instead of blaming the microbes, people looked for noxious gases called miasmas.
2) Louis Pasteur was employed in 1857 to find the explanation for the souring of sugar beet used in fermenting industrial alcohol. His answer was to blame germs in the air. He proved there were germs in the air by sterilising some water and keeping it in a flask that didn't allow airborne particles to enter. This stayed sterile — but sterilised water kept in an open flask bred micro-organisms again.

After such a great start Pasteur was blighted by some serious bad luck. His father and two of his daughters died, then he suffered a stroke that left him partially paralysed. He stopped working. From 1870-1871 Pasteur's country, France, fought a war against Prussia and was badly beaten. Then a German started to develop his ideas. Sacré bleu!

Robert Koch used dyes to identify microbes

1) Gradually improving his methods, Robert Koch began the process of linking diseases to the microbe that caused them. He developed a solid medium to grow cultures, and dyeing techniques to colour microbes, which he viewed through high-powered microscopes. He used his daughter's pet mice to experiment with.
2) He identified anthrax spores (1875) and the bacteria that cause septicaemia, tuberculosis (1882) and cholera (1883).

Koch-a-leekie — my favourite antipasteur...

Pasteur's germ theory was a monumental breakthrough — and the springboard for all the other developments in this section. Remember that none of these breakthroughs came straight out of the blue — they all built on the work of others before them — usually many others. Even Pasteur's work would have been impossible without things like the microscope.

Vaccines and Antitoxins

Fuelled by ambition and personal rivalries, the race for further discoveries was on.

Pasteur, champion of France, finds chicken cholera vaccine

1) Hearing of Koch's work, Pasteur came out of retirement in 1877 and started to compete in the race to find new microbes and combat them. The defeat of France spurred him on.
2) Many other scientists joined this new field of bacteriology.
3) Pasteur looked for cures to anthrax and chicken cholera. Both he and Koch had been given large teams in this national competition. Charles Chamberland was in Pasteur's team.
4) One day Chamberland was told to inject some chickens with chicken cholera, but it was the day before his holiday, and he forgot (as you do). He left the cholera culture on his desk,

and injected the chickens when he returned (no-one will notice, right?) The chickens survived. They tried again with some newly cultured cholera, but the chickens still survived.

5) They worked out that the cholera had been weakened by being left on the desk for a few days, and that the weakened (attenuated) cholera had made the chickens immune — in the same way that Jenner's cowpox vaccine had worked for smallpox. Chamberland's error had produced a chance discovery.

Vaccines for Anthrax and Rabies soon followed

1) Pasteur's team returned to anthrax and managed to produce an attenuated version of the spore that would make sheep immune. They demonstrated this in a public experiment in 1881.
2) Next on their hit list was rabies. Emile Roux had used dried rabbit spines to discover how long the rabies microbe remained dangerous. Pasteur borrowed (OK, nicked) Roux's idea to create a series of inoculations of increasing virulence (liveliness). He hoped these would lead to immunity.

3) Things were looking pretty good when a distraught woman arrived with her son, who had been horribly bitten by a rabid dog. Knowing that the child was bound to die if nothing was done, Pasteur agreed to try out the new treatment on him. Fortunately, the treatment worked.

Vaccines before an illness? What if you're already ill...

1) The diphtheria germ had been discovered by Edwin Klebs in 1882.
2) Freidrich Loeffler cultured the germs and thought that their effect on people was due to a poison or toxin they produced.
3) Emile Roux proved Loeffler right and then in 1891 Emil von Behring produced an antitoxin or serum from the blood of animals that had just recovered from diphtheria. This could be used to reduce the effect of the disease.

Goodbye to germs — Pasteur la vista, baby...

Lots more facts here I'm afraid — and they're important. As usual, try to see the bigger picture — think how the facts relate to other areas of medicine, and try to judge their importance and role in the history of medicine. Think which of the key factors apply here. Even war was important — because it helped to fuel Pasteur and Koch's legendary rivalry.

Sulphonamides and Penicillin

The diphtheria antitoxin was only the first of many effective cures found by modern science.

Paul Erlich found a chemical treatment for syphilis

1) Paul Ehrlich set out to find chemicals that could act as synthetic antibodies. Antibodies had been identified as a natural defence mechanism of the body by Metchnikoff in 1884. It was known that antibodies attacked specific microbes (hence they were called magic bullets). As part of Koch's team, Ehrlich had previously used dyes to stain microbes. He now started to see if some of those dyes could kill germs.

2) He discovered dyes that could kill the malaria and sleeping sickness germs.

3) For many years arsenic or mercury had been used with some success to treat the sexually transmitted disease syphilis. Unfortunately arsenic and mercury are both poisonous, so it was a fine line between cure and kill. In 1906 the spirochete bacterium that causes syphilis was identified — prompting a search for an arsenic compound that was a magic bullet for syphilis.

Magic bullet or second assassin on grassy knoll?

4) Over 600 compounds were tried, but none seemed to work. Then a new worker joined the team in 1909 called Sahachiro Hata. He was given the task of rechecking the results for the compounds already tested. Surprisingly he found that one of them, number 606, did appear to work. It was first used on a human in 1911 under the trade name Salvarsan 606.

Work on dyes was continuing, but nature and chance were about to make a major contribution.

Fleming discovered penicillin — the first antibiotic

1) The discovery of penicillin is a great example of a chance finding helping science.

2) Alexander Fleming saw many soldiers die of septic wounds caused by staphylococci bacteria when he was working in an army hospital during the First World War.

3) Searching for a cure he identified the antiseptic substance in tears, lysozyme, in 1922 — but this only worked on some germs.

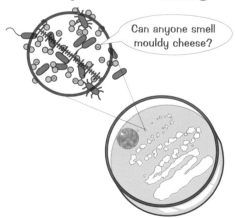

Can anyone smell mouldy cheese?

4) One day in 1928 he came to clean up some old culture dishes on which he had been growing staphylococci for his experiments. By chance a fungal spore had landed and grown on one of the dishes.

5) What caught Fleming's eye was that the colonies of staphylococci around the mould had stopped growing. The fungus was identified as *Penicillium notatum*. It produced a substance that killed bacteria. The substance was given the name penicillin.

6) Fleming was unable to take his work further. The industrial production of penicillin still needed to be developed.

Ehrlich in the morning, when the dye was dawning...

Paul Ehrlich's work was basically trial and error, based on a hunch. The fact that so many different compounds were tested is some measure of his perseverance — a key quality of all these scientists. Chance played a big role in Ehrlich's discovery, but probably not as much as in Fleming's. When you think you know the facts, cover the page, note them down, then check.

Sulphonamides and Penicillin

There were lots more surprises to come — including another dye-hard and pure penicillin.

Gerhard Domagk found a dye that stopped strepococci

1) Gerhard Domagk had already had success in discovering a cure for sleeping sickness when in 1932 he found that a red dye, prontosil, stopped the streptococcus microbe from multiplying in mice — without being poisonous to the mice. Streptococcus caused a frequently fatal blood poisoning that could be contracted from very minor wounds. Many surgeons contracted it after cutting themselves in the operating theatre.

Just tell them you've been on holiday to Majorca.

2) In 1935 Hildegarde, Domagk's daughter, pricked herself with a needle and caught the disease. Afraid she would die, Domagk gave her a large dose of prontosil. The girl turned bright red, but recovered.

3) The active ingredient of prontosil was identified as a sulphonamide by French scientists. A whole group of drugs based on sulphonamides followed, including M&B 693, which worked on pneumonia without turning you any strange colour.

4) Alas, more serious side-effects were later discovered. Sulphonamide drugs can damage your liver and kidneys.

Florey and Chain found a way to purify penicillin

1) Being a natural product, penicillin needed purifying. The breakthrough was made by Howard Florey's team in Oxford between 1938 and 1940. Ernst Chain devised the freeze-drying technique, though they didn't have the resources to produce penicillin in large amounts.

2) They produced penicillin for the first clinical trial by growing Penicillium notatum in every container they could find in their lab. The patient began to recover, only to die when the penicillin ran out.

3) Florey knew that penicillin could be vital in treating the wounds being received by soldiers at the time (WWII). British chemical firms were too busy making explosives to start mass production — so he went to America.

4) American firms were not keen to help before America joined the war in 1941. By 1944 mass production was sufficient for the needs of the military medics.
(An early recipient, who contracted a chest infection serving on anti-aircraft guns, was Jack Atkinson — my grandad.)

5) Fleming, Florey and Chain were awarded the Nobel Prize in 1945.

A cure for all ills? — not Fleming likely...

Yet another example of war helping to advance medicine. And another use of dyes. The stuff on penicillin's really important. Make sure you understand the effect it had on medicine. But don't forget it was no use in minute quantities — so technology was essential for its production. Just think what a difference that would have made in earlier centuries.

Anaesthetics

Pain, bleeding and infection were the three bugbears of surgery.
Trouble is, they were kind of solved in the wrong order.

Anaesthetics made life easier for all concerned

1) The use of natural drugs like alcohol, opium and mandrake to reduce pain was long established — but effective anaesthetics that didn't make the patient very ill were more difficult to produce until the chemical industry flourished.

2) Nitrous oxide (laughing gas) was identified as a possible anaesthetic by Humphry Davy in 1799 — but he was ignored by surgeons of the time.

3) In 1842, Crawford Long didn't publicise his discovery of the anaesthetic qualities of ether.

4) Nitrous oxide had been relegated to use as a fairground novelty when Horace Wells suggested its use in dentistry. He did a public demonstration in 1845, but had the terrible luck (chance factor) to pick a patient unaffected by the gas — and nitrous oxide was again ignored.

5) In 1846, after persuasion by William Morton, John Warren did a public demonstration of the use of ether.

6) Ether is an irritant and is also fairly explosive, so there were risks. In 1847 James Simpson undertook self-experimentation that amounted to solvent abuse — but in a good cause. He discovered the effects of chloroform.

What was it we were looking for again?

7) Chloroform turned out to cause liver damage, leading to a return to ether.

8) General anaesthesia (complete unconsciousness) was and still is risky, so local anaesthesia (numbing of the part treated) is better for many operations. In 1884, William Halsted investigated the use of cocaine as a local anaesthetic. However, his self-experimentation led to a severe cocaine addiction.

New anaesthetics were not entirely a good thing

1) Some people were suspicious of doctors using anaesthetics — or even objected on religious grounds. Others were afraid of side effects and the dangers of overdose.

2) Surgeons were keen to perform more and more complicated operations because an unconscious patient was cooperative and the surgeon could take longer over his work.

3) As the dangers of bleeding and infection had not been overcome, the attempts at more complicated surgery actually led to increased death rates amongst patients. "The operation was a success but the patient died," is a famous saying that sums up the position at this stage. The period between 1846 and 1870 is sometimes called the "Black Period" of surgery.

4) Modern anaesthetists use complicated mixtures to produce muscle relaxation or paralysis. Getting the balance of the different drugs right is tricky — it has been known for patients to be paralysed, unable to cry out, but fully conscious and in excruciating pain.

Anaesthetics — learn your stuff and it won't hurt a bit...

Anaesthetics were definitely a major advance, but don't forget about that grisly "Black Period" — and what caused it. You should be able to recite the facts in your sleep, but you're not allowed anaesthetic for the exam. Try learning the stuff factor by factor — first the people, then the communications, then the bits on religion, technology etc. It's practice for "organise and deploy".

Antisepsis and Asepsis

Luckily, methods to reduce infection soon followed. There's two types of approach.

Joseph Lister pioneered antiseptic methods

1) Antiseptic methods kill germs that get near the surgical wound. Aseptic methods aim to stop any germs getting near the surgical wound.
2) Before Pasteur's germ theory, infection was thought to be due to miasmas (unhealthy gases) in the air — or dust particles.
3) Ignaz Semmelweis had used chloride of lime solution as a hand wash for doctors to control the spread of puerperal fever, an infection suffered by many women following childbirth. However, it was very unpleasant, so wasn't widely used.

J. Lister

4) Joseph Lister had seen carbolic acid sprays used in sewage works to keep down the smell. He tried this in the operating theatre in the early 1860s and saw reduced infection rates. Having heard about the germ theory in 1865, he realised that germs could be in the air and on surgical instruments and people's hands. He started using carbolic acid on instruments and bandages. This produced further improvements.
5) Carbolic acid is unpleasant to get on your skin or breathe in — so many doctors and nurses didn't like or use it.
6) The use of antiseptic conditions reduced death rates from as high as 50% to about 15%. By 1890 antiseptics were being used by most European and American surgeons.

Asepsis reduced the need for nasty chemicals

1) By going from killing germs to making a germ-free environment, surgeons have been able to avoid using large amounts of antiseptic in the theatre.
2) Instruments are carefully sterilised before use, usually with high temperature steam (120°C). The prions (rogue proteins) that cause BSE and its human equivalent, CJD, are capable of surviving higher temperatures — so more disposable instruments are now used on tissues that could contain prions.
3) Operating theatre staff sterilise their hands before entering — and wear sterile gowns, masks, gloves and hats. Surgical gloves were invented by William Halsted in 1889.
4) The theatres themselves are kept scrupulously clean and fed with sterile air. Special tents can be placed around the operating table to maintain an area of even stricter hygiene in high risk cases.

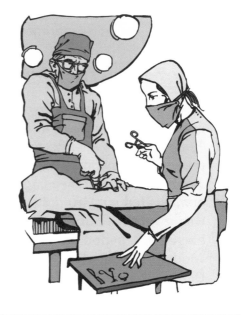

Make a Lister them facts — then germ up on them...

Right, a couple of tricky words here. The key to the page is to understand the difference between "antiseptic" and "aseptic". Of course you do need to know about the methods used as well. Remember that Lister started using carbolic acid before he'd heard about the germ theory. He was able to improve his methods later when he understood how they worked.

Blood Transfusion, X-rays and Keyhole Sugery

Blood transfusions, radiography and keyhole surgery have revolutionised 20th century medicine.

Karl Landsteiner discovered blood groups in 1900

1) Blood circulates rapidly, so it doesn't take long to bleed to death if a major blood vessel is cut. Surgery often causes heavy bleeding.
2) The concept of blood transfusions was known from at least the 17th century, when Jean-Baptiste Denys made a transfusion between dogs and Richard Lower carried out a cross-species transfusion to a human (1667).
3) The problem was that sometimes it worked and sometimes the blood of the recipient clogged, they died and no-one knew why.
4) In 1900 Karl Landsteiner discovered blood groups and the importance of compatibility.
5) During the First World War sodium citrate was found to stop clotting when blood came into contact with the air. This allowed blood to be stored more easily.
6) In 1938 the British National Blood Transfusion Service was established.

X-rays and Radiography — look before you cut

1) X-rays were discovered by Wilhelm Roentgen in 1895. They pass easily through soft flesh, but less well through bone. They also affect photographic film. These factors allow simple X-ray images to be produced by directing X-rays at a body part in front of a photographic plate.
2) Several major improvements were made that are worth noting. The intestines don't usually show up in an X-ray, but if barium meal is eaten, which absorbs X-rays, it becomes visible. X-ray-absorbing dyes can be injected into the bloodstream to follow blood flow. In computerized axial tomography (CAT), a scanner rotates 180° around the body, aiming thin beams of X-rays at receptors on the opposite side of the person. A computer analyses the results and produces an image of a slice of the body. The slices can be built up into a 3D image of the body.

H. Becquerel

M. Curie

3) Between 1896 and 1898 Antoine Henri Becquerel and Pierre and Marie Curie discovered the first radioactive isotopes. Radioactive isotopes are used in diagnosis as tracers, in radiotherapy and in immunosuppression (see the bit on transplant surgery).

Keyhole Surgery is also good for investigating illness

1) Keyhole surgery is a modern technique (developed in the 1980s) which allows surgery to be less invasive. It's popular with patients because scars are smaller and recovery is quicker.
2) In keyhole surgery, a surgical instrument is put through a small cut of about 1 to 2cm. It gives out light and feeds back a picture to a screen, letting the surgeon see inside the body.
3) Other instruments are needed for the actual surgery, which are introduced through even smaller cuts in the skin. Keyhole surgery is usually performed under a general anaesthetic.
4) This technique is useful for investigating the causes of pain or infertility. It's also used for sterilisations, removing cysts or the appendix, mending hernias and other minor operations.

Blood confusion? — grouping around in the dark...

Don't forget that governments often play key roles in discoveries — they supply the money to fund the research. And government spending is often heavily influenced by social attitudes.

Transplants and Repair

Like keyhole surgery, many other surgical techniques came of age in the last half-century.

Transplants — a brand new branch of surgery

1) Replacing worn out body parts is something we're still just beginning to get the hang of. Mechanical parts are quite common now for joint replacement and prosthetic (artificial) limbs, but artificial vital organs cannot compare to the real thing. Transplant surgery using donor organs has usually been the only option.
2) The first organ to be transplanted was the kidney (in 1951), closely followed by the cornea of the eye.
3) Livers, lungs, pancreases and bone marrow are also transplanted, but the organ that has excited most interest has always been the heart. Apart from rejection problems, you also have to keep the body supplied with blood and oxygen, then get the new heart to beat after the operation. And most heart disease patients have additional problems with other parts of the cardiovascular system and other organs.
4) Heart transplantation became a bit of a race amongst heart surgeons. The three people chasing the glory of being first were Norman Shumway, Adrian Kantrowitz and Christiaan Barnard. The winner was Barnard who carried out the first heart transplant on 3rd December 1967. The patient survived only 18 days.
5) The poor life expectancy of patients soon led to a temporary cessation of heart transplants.
6) The major problem for any transplant is rejection, which is when the host body's immune system attacks the implant. The immune system has to be suppressed until the implant is accepted as part of the "home team".
7) At first corticosteroids were used as immunosuppressants — but they often stopped all resistance to diseases like pneumonia. In 1983 cyclosporin was developed, a fungus-derived drug which has since been used successfully with many patients. A fungus was also the source of tacrolimus (FK506), a further immunosuppressant drug developed in 1994.

Wars sped the development of Plastic surgery

1) Twentieth century warfare tends to produce a higher proportion of burn injuries than in previous centuries. Aircraft especially, but also tanks and ships, have a worrying tendency to catch fire with people trapped inside.
2) Skin grafting had been known in Rennaisance Europe and since ancient times in India — but infection had limited its usefulness.
3) Harold Gillies began working with burns victims from the First World War. His work was continued during the Second World War by his assistant, Archibald McIndoe — probably the most famous plastic surgeon ever.
4) McIndoe's unit in East Grinstead took advantage of new developments in antibacterial drugs and surgical techniques. They also worked very hard to help their patients through the psychological effects of their injuries.

Plastic surgery — it's no skin off my nose...

Don't forget advances like these always build on past advances. You might have to compare advances at different times, so it's best to get some practice in now. Think of the similarities and differences — think which factors they had in common. And when you think you know the key bits, turn over the page and scribble them down — then check you've got them all.

SECTION TEN — THE DEVELOPMENT OF MODERN SURGERY

City Slums and Cholera

Medieval and Renaissance towns had failed to reach the standards of public health seen in Roman times — but the Industrial Revolution made things even worse.

The Industrial Revolution was bad for your health

1) The towns of the medieval period were not densely packed with rows and rows of buildings as we see them today. Within a town there were gardens for growing vegetables and keeping pigs and chickens. There were also orchards of fruit trees.
2) Industry and changes in agriculture brought more people into the towns. The spaces filled up with factories and poor quality housing. Anyone who owned land could build on it without planning permission — and there were no building standards regulations.
3) People didn't believe the government had the right to tell people what to do with their land. They expected "no-intervention" policies from the government (laissez-faire).
4) Attempts at providing fresh water and removing sewage and rubbish were totally inadequate. Sewage was discharged into rivers, overflowing cesspits or even into the street. Smoke from houses and factories filled the air. Dangerous chemicals escaped from many factories.
5) Smallpox, influenza, typhus and typhoid fever were common.

Cholera — an epidemic within a year of arrival

1) Cholera reached Britain from the East in 1831, and was an epidemic by 1832.
2) Cholera spreads when infected sewage gets into drinking water. It causes such extreme diarrhoea that sufferers often die from loss of water and minerals. Both rich and poor people caught the disease.
3) The Government started to introduce regulations about the burial of the dead, but the epidemic declined and interest was lost.
4) People did not know what caused cholera. Epidemics recurred in 1848, 1854 and 1866.

Chadwick was ignored — until the next outbreak

1) Chadwick published a "Report on the Sanitary Condition of the Labouring Population of Great Britain" in 1842. His revolutionary idea was that improved public health provision and a healthy workforce would save money rather than cost money. The report and statistics describing levels of sickness and mortality shocked some of the privileged classes.
2) The Clean Party campaigned for improvements, and in 1844 the Health of Towns Association was set up.
3) Responding to calls from the Health of Towns Association, the government introduced a Public Health Bill. It was opposed by the "Dirty Party". The bill was finally passed when a new cholera epidemic broke out. It became the first Public Health Act, in 1848.
4) The main provision of the act was for Central and local Health Boards. The local boards had to be approved by ratepayers, and the Central Board lasted until it was dismantled in 1854.

Learn the facts — give your brain a clean bill of health...

OK, so basically the Industrial Revolution was a time of very poor living conditions for lots of workers. There were loads of large towns without sanitation or clean water. And surprise surprise, there were epidemics. Chadwick's report was a landmark. Make sure you understand why it was so important — and the factors that lead to the poor conditions in the first place.

The Defeat of Laissez-Faire

John Snow linked cholera to contaminated water, while more voices joined the call for action.

Snow linked cholera to contaminated water

1) The connection between contaminated water and cholera was discovered by John Snow in 1854.
2) He plotted the occurrence of a cholera outbreak in the Broad Street area of London and noticed that the victims all used the same water pump. So he removed the handle from the pump — and ended the outbreak.

The 1860s and 70s saw the defeat of laissez-faire

1) Chadwick and Snow were finally proved right when Pasteur discovered germs.
2) In 1871 and 1872 the government responded to proposals of the Medical Officer of Health, Sir John Simon, by forming the Local Government Board and dividing the country into "sanitary areas" administered by medical officers of health.
3) The second Public Health Act was brought in by Disraeli's government in 1875, along with the Artisans' Dwellings Act. The 1875 act was more effective than the first one because it forced local councils to act on public health.
4) The Artisans' Dwellings Act allowed for compulsory purchase of slum housing and rebuilding by local councils (although the act was seldom used). This act owed much to the work of Octavia Hill, who was concerned with the terrible conditions in which people were living and so developed a model housing scheme. Octavia Hill was also determined that people should have access to green spaces for their health and well-being. She campaigned to save open spaces from being built on and ended up co-founding the National Trust in 1895.
5) Victorian Engineering produced improvements in the form of brick-lined sewer networks and steam-driven pumped water systems — such as the Boughton Pumping Station.

Philanthropists and soldiers sang the same song

1) Think of a Victorian businessman and most of us see a cruel exploiter of the masses, sipping champagne whilst small children get mangled in steam-driven machinery.
2) There was, however, the other side of the coin. The shipping owner Charles Booth surveyed living conditions in London's East End and published "Life and Labour of the People" in 1903. A similar survey was made in York by Seebolm Rowntree, of the chocolate family.
3) The other famous chocolate makers, the Cadburys, tried to create a utopia of quality homes and improved lifestyles around their factory in Bournville, near Birmingham. Titus Salt did a similar thing in Saltaire (c.1850) in Yorkshire.
4) These philanthropist businessmen were great examples of how to make money and treat your workers well, even if they did sip champagne too.
5) When the Boer War broke out in 1902, army officers found that 40% of volunteers were unfit for military service — mostly due to poverty-related illnesses linked with poor diet and living conditions. Similar problems were encountered during the First World War. Britain, like the Romans, realised it needed a healthy population to have an efficient army.

Snow use ignoring them — those germs won't go away...

Make sure you understand why change took so long. Firstly, there was much less communication, so many people were ignorant of the conditions. And secondly, there was the belief in laissez-faire.

Liberal Reforms and Women's Rights

The Liberal government elected in 1906 was the first to make many important changes.

Liberal Government Reforms — Social Security measures

1) From 1906 the Liberal government started to introduce measures that are still important to our social security today: Free school meals — 1906,
School medical inspections — 1907,
Old Age Pension Act — 1909,
Labour Exchanges (Job Centres) — 1909,
National Insurance Act — 1911.
Lloyd George had to overcome great opposition from the House of Lords to get many of these reforms through.

David Lloyd George

2) National Insurance wasn't compulsory and it only covered people who paid in.   These could then get sick pay and medical treatment from a "panel doctor" working for the scheme.
Many couldn't afford to pay National Insurance. The scheme also provided unemployment pay.

Women had to fight to re-enter the medical profession

1) Women were not able to attend universities in the early 19th century. Consequently they could not qualify as doctors. Many Victorian men regarded women as being less able to work in jobs requiring professionalism, intelligence or lack of squeamishness.
2) Some women lived their lives pretending to be men to pursue a career. Miranda Stewart Barry was born in 1797 and trained at Edinburgh University as "James Barrie". She qualified at the age of 15 in 1812, and joined the Army in time to serve at the Battle of Waterloo where she was promoted to Assistant Surgeon. She became Inspector General of Hospitals in 1858 and practised for a total of 53 years, only being found out when she died in 1865.
3) Elizabeth Blackwell (an English-born American) was the first woman in "modern times" to be awarded a medical degree in her own name from a western training college (1849).
4) The first British women to practise openly as qualified modern doctors both had to train privately or abroad. Elizabeth Garrett Anderson was trained privately before being accepted as a qualified doctor by the Society of Apothecaries in 1865. She used the society's rules to force it to recognise her — but afterwards they changed their rules to stop other women doing the same. She was awarded a medical degree by the University of Paris in 1870.
Sophia Jex-Blake gained entry to Edinburgh University, but was refused a degree when her entry was declared unlawful. She then founded the London School of Medicine for Women in 1874, and gained her own qualification from the University of Bern in Switzerland.
5) The need for women in professional roles increased during the world wars.
6) The 1975 Sex Discrimination Act meant, in theory, that equal opportunities should be available in almost all jobs.
7) Today women are still under-represented in the medical professions — especially in more promoted posts like hospital consultants.

Lloyd George — wasn't he in Culture Club?...

All those laws at the top of the page are really important stuff. Make sure you understand just how big a breakthrough they were. Also don't forget there was loads of opposition to them — especially from rich lords, with the most to lose. The things that held women back were different, but it's equally important you understand them. Think what factors held women back, and what ones allowed them to succeed. And as usual, learn the stuff, turn the page, then scribble it down.

SECTION ELEVEN — RECENT ADVANCES IN PUBLIC HEALTH

The National Health Service

The setting up of the NHS was a great achievement of the post-war government.

War points towards NHS and Welfare State

1) The world wars broke down social distinctions and brought people together whose lives had been very separate. The raising of mass armies made powerful people take notice of the health problems of the poor. Also the evacuation of children during the Second World War increased awareness in rural middle England of how disadvantaged many people were.

2) After both world wars people had looked for improvements in society — "a land fit for heroes". Such feelings led to the 1945 victory for the Labour Party. They campaigned with the slogan "Cheer for Churchill, Vote for Labour" — calling for change whilst acknowledging the debt Britain owed to the wartime leadership of Churchill. He was hoping to be re-elected as Conservative prime minister.

3) Air raids, especially the Blitz of 1940, prompted the government to set up the Emergency Medical Service. This provided a centralised control of medical services and offered free treatment to air raid casualties. It proved successful under great pressure.

Bevan introduced the NHS following the Beveridge Report

1) Sir William Beveridge published his famous Beveridge Report in 1942. In it he called for the state provision of social security "from the cradle to the grave".

2) The report became a bestseller. In it Beveridge argued that all people should have the right to be free from want, disease, ignorance, squalor and idleness. He called these the five "giants".

3) Aneurin Bevan was the Labour Minister for Health who introduced the National Health Service.

4) Compulsory National Insurance was introduced in 1948 to pay for the NHS. Doctors and dentists were wooed with a fixed payment for each registered patient. They were also allowed to continue treating private fee-paying patients.

5) By 1948 nearly all hospitals had joined the NHS and 92% of doctors had.

A rational health service — the well fair state?...

OK, it's NHS time. It tends to get taken for granted these days, but you've got to remember it hasn't been around that long. It was a major turning point, so make sure you know the factors that led to its formation, and why they were important. Start with these — the Liberal Government 1906-14, social attitudes, the Beveridge report, the Labour victory and the war.

NHS Crises, Alternatives and the WHO

Trouble is, the NHS proved a bit expensive, and many problems have got worse in recent years.

The NHS has had Problems from the start

1) Right from the start the demand for NHS services was greater than expected. In 1950 spending was about £350 million — twice the expected. By 1960 it was £726 million.

2) Over the years since the War things have got more difficult. Medical research has produced more and more complex machines and more expensive drugs. Success in the form of longer life expectancies has meant more need for care of the elderly.

3) NHS problems over health service "rationing" can be best appreciated by considering a hypothetical example. Imagine a treatment were invented tomorrow which, when carried out on babies, would make them immune to all forms of cancer. Great! Unfortunately it costs £2 million per child. What do you do? Ban it entirely, make it available only for the very rich, make it the prize in the National Lottery — or bankrupt the country?

4) Successive governments have reduced how much of the NHS is free — charges have been reintroduced for things like prescriptions and dental checkups. Aneurin Bevan resigned over prescription charges. Long waiting lists and doubts about the quality of treatment have led many to take out private health insurance, or pay for treatment outside the NHS.

Is High-Tech always best?

1) Thalidomide, BSE, E-coli, MMR vaccines and cancer clusters have all increased concern and even paranoia over high-tech agriculture, industry and medicine. These are worth investigating as part of broader revision.

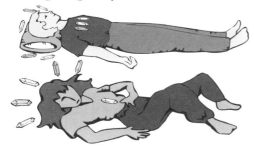

2) Recent years have seen a resurgence of interest in "alternative", "traditional" or even supernatural forms of health care. Few doctors would dispute the success of many of these treatments — even if they attribute their success to faith, or the placebo effect — rather than the power of crystals, auras etc.

Health for the Global Village

1) The World Health Organisation (WHO) was set up in 1948 as part of the United Nations. It has been very successful in increasing the number of children vaccinated worldwide.

2) Its other major success was the total eradication of smallpox. It also works hard trying to eliminate polio, malaria and tuberculosis.

NHS — National High Spenders?...

The NHS might have been a major success, but remember it's never been without its problems. And these have got worse by the year. The main thing here is to understand the reasons for the problems, and their effects. Money has always been a major factor of course, and scientific and technological breakthroughs have made this far worse. Don't forget though that money's not the only problem — things like bureaucracy and inefficiency have contributed too.

Where to from Here?

Many recent advances have been based on genetics — so you'd best learn a bit about it.

DNA and genetics — a continuing development

J.Watson + F.Crick

1) The understanding of inheritance has been a slow development going back into prehistory — to whenever someone noticed that children looked a bit like their parents and could inherit characteristics from them.

2) The structure of DNA was first described in 1953 by Francis Crick and James Watson. They relied heavily on the work of Rosalind Franklin and Maurice Wilkins. All except Franklin shared in the 1962 Nobel Prize for Physiology or Medicine. Rosalind Franklin had died four years earlier in 1958.

3) The structure of DNA is a double helix (a kind of spiral) which can reproduce itself by splitting. DNA forms a coded message detailing the characteristics of the plant or animal from which it comes. This genetic information is passed from cell to cell and generation to generation.

4) Genetic engineering has been around since prehistory in the form of selective breeding. It has now accelerated as scientists have learnt to manipulate individual genes and splice different genes together to give genetically modified organisms (GMOs). This has led to worries about the safety and ethics of research.

Who are you calling Genetically Modified?

5) The Human Genome Project has identified all the genes in human DNA. The task was huge as there are between 20,000 and 25,000 genes. Scientists are now in the process of analysing the results.

6) Not all modern developments are progress. Overuse of antibiotics is leading to the evolution of superbugs which are resistant to our antibacterial drugs. Fear of side effects (which all drugs have) lead some people to reject vaccinations, despite the risks of the diseases being greater than those of the vaccines against them.

The Human Gnome Project — it might improve our elf...

Lots of science and technology here, that's for sure. But don't forget there's many other relevant factors. Take communications and governments. Without governments clubbing together with a bit of cash, little scientific research would get done — especially stuff like this where any applications might be a long way in the future. Also, government-funded research tends to get shared more. Companies, on the other hand, like to keep things to themselves.

History of Childbirth

A change of scene now — time for a look at <u>childbirth</u> through the ages.

We <u>humans</u> aren't designed for an <u>easy birth</u>

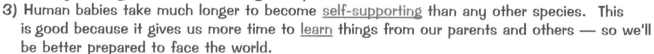

1) <u>Wildlife programmes</u> often show newborn animals and their mothers running about just hours after birth. There are several reasons why you don't see that sort of thing with <u>humans</u>.

2) Being bipeds puts extra strain on our backs and pelvis which is made worse during pregnancy. Another problem is our <u>heads</u> are <u>too big</u>. They're about as big as they could get and still fit through the pelvis.

3) Human babies take much longer to become <u>self-supporting</u> than any other species. This is good because it gives us more time to <u>learn</u> things from our parents and others — so we'll be better prepared to face the world.

4) Humans, especially in recent history, have not been as <u>athletically fit</u> and active as they might have been. This is mainly because our jobs tend to involve <u>sedentary</u> "work". Most other species do a lot more <u>running about</u> as part of their everyday activities.

5) Many female mammals <u>work together</u> in caring for groups of young after birth. It's likely <u>humans</u> have done similar things (midwifery and wet-nursing) right from the start of <u>prehistory</u>.

Midwifery, obstetrics and gynaecology — useful words...

1) <u>Midwifery</u> is what a <u>midwife</u> does — it's the branch of <u>nursing</u> that helps with <u>childbirth</u>.

2) <u>Obstetrics</u> is the branch of <u>medicine</u> that covers <u>childbirth</u> — so it includes midwifery.

3) <u>Gynaecology</u> is the branch of medicine that deals with problems specific to <u>women</u>, but <u>not</u> including obstetrics. It covers things like infertility and menstrual problems.

Ancient Egypt had midwives and doctors

1) There is some evidence that male <u>priest doctors</u> sometimes assisted with childbirth in Egypt — but there are also surviving <u>wall paintings</u> showing women alone assisting at a birth.

2) The "<u>Papyrus Kahun</u>" describes the diagnosis and treatment of a "falling womb", so it is clear that <u>gynaecology</u> was practised by the priest doctors.

The Greeks and Romans trained their midwives

1) <u>Greek and Roman</u> midwives were <u>taught</u> by doctors. A doctor was called in if any <u>problem</u> developed with a pregnancy.

MacDuff was from his mother's womb untimely ripp'd.

2) The best known obstetric operation, the <u>Caesarean section</u>, originates from the Lex Caesarea — a law of the <u>9th century BC</u>. It said that if a pregnant woman died, the foetus should be removed and <u>buried separately</u> from the mother. The date of the first Caesarean to leave the mother and child alive is unknown.

Learn about childbirth — don't have a midwife crisis...

OK, so our brains are <u>too big</u>. Unfortunately, size isn't everything. What you learn and how you use knowledge is what counts. Use some of that space to learn those <u>fancy words</u>. Remember that what we know of childbirth through the ages is pretty <u>patchy</u> — so we often have to <u>infer</u> things from pictures and stuff. Now learn the <u>details</u> and <u>scribble</u> them down.

Childbirth in the Middle Ages

The Middle Ages and Renaissance saw little development of ideas on childbirth.

Medieval Arabs and Christians had childbirth specialists

1) The early Islamic Arabs had female doctors who assisted in obstetrics and gynaecology.
2) In the Christian West midwives developed an apprenticeship approach to training, which was completely separate from the training of doctors in the developing universities. There was little connection between the two until the 16th century.

The Renaissance saw slow progress

1) Ambroise Paré, who is most famous for his work on gunshot wounds and amputations, also covered pregnancy in a book on surgery — mind you, he did record 35 live children from one pregnancy. Yeah, right. Eucharius Rösslin wrote the earliest surviving book on midwifery in 1513.
2) The French Chamberlens family invented specialised obstetric forceps. They brought them to England when they fled religious persecution in 16th century France.
3) Male midwives (accoucheurs) became fashionable amongst the elite in 17th century France. As with most high fashion, the majority of people stuck to the more traditional option.
4) The medical profession became more interested in obstetrics in the 18th century, and the first British school of midwifery opened in 1725. William Smellie published "The theory and Practice of Midwifery". Traditional midwives were sceptical of his writings.

5) Childbirth was a very dangerous activity. Gravestones and registers of deaths from the Renaissance period onwards show how many women died in their twenties during or soon after pregnancy.
6) There were leather condoms in the 17th century and earlier, but the lack of effective widely available contraception before the 20th century made chastity the only effective family planning.

Children — I give them a wide birth myself...

Remember that the Renaissance was a rebirth of interest in the old classical ideas of the Greeks and Romans — although it didn't have that much effect on midwifery. Notice how midwifery has often been taught and practised completely separately from other areas of medicine. Think about the reasons for this, and how social attitudes have played a part in its development.

SECTION ELEVEN — RECENT ADVANCES IN PUBLIC HEALTH

Population Growth and Family Planning

Big improvements were made from the Industrial Revolution onwards.

Industrial Revolution — mass (re)production

1) The industrial age saw a huge rise in the population growth.
2) This was despite the poor conditions in cities, which made women less likely to survive a normal pregnancy. Lack of exercise, pollution-related diseases and deficiency diseases like rickets all weakened the people.
3) Epidemics of smallpox, tuberculosis and cholera not only killed many, but left people weakened.
4) Some people raised religious objections to using anaesthetics in childbirth. They thought part of Genesis said women were meant to suffer pain during childbirth. These voices (how much do you want to bet most were male?) were only really defeated when Queen Victoria asked for chloroform during the birth of Prince Leopold.

> Giving birth without anaesthetic? We are not amused!

5) The development of antiseptics did a lot to reduce the deaths of women following childbirth — especially Semmelweis's use of chloride of lime to control post-natal puerperal fever.
6) Gynaecology as a separate branch of surgery dates from the mid-1800s, with much of the pioneering work being done in America. J.M. Simms opened the first gynaecological hospital in New York in the 1840s.

Family planning help had to wait till the 20th century

1) In 1798 Thomas Robert Malthus was the first to suggest that the human species might increase in numbers beyond its ability to feed itself.
2) The reduction of deaths in childbirth meant an increased rate of population growth — and a greater need for family planning.
3) Clinics providing barrier and chemical forms of contraception and family planning advice were pioneered in the 1920s — by Marie Stopes in Britain and Margaret Sanger in America.
4) Contraceptive pills first appeared in the late 1950s. For a while the pill and effective antibiotics seemed to offer security from unwanted pregnancy and sexually-transmitted disease. This helped fuel the sexual revolution of the 1960s. HIV changed that.
5) The World Health Organisation and the UN Population Fund have been working to bring effective family planning to the developing world.

> And they call us vermin...

It Simms if I don't Stopes soon, I'll get born away...

Queen Victoria's decision to use chloroform was one of those major turning points you need to know about. That's what was needed to change the social and religious attitudes of the day. Communications were also important though — without them, there'd have been no debate, and few people would have known of the Queen's actions — or of chloroform for that matter.

SECTION ELEVEN — RECENT ADVANCES IN PUBLIC HEALTH

Some Recent Developments

Unfortunately, it's not all rosy. A number of recent developments have led to controversies.

HIV, AIDS and more — Problems for the new century

1) HIV (Human Immunodeficiency Virus) is thought to have originated in Africa, but the disease it causes (AIDS — Acquired Immune Deficiency Syndrome) was first identified in America in 1981.
2) AIDS is an even bigger problem in the developing world — especially in Africa. Levels of infection are staggering in some areas. The WHO is coordinating efforts to look for vaccines and cures. Several approaches have been trialled, but as yet without much success.

Infertility and Impotency treatments

The Proud Parents

1) New infertility treatments have recently been developed.
2) Most famous is IVF (in vitro fertilisation — or test-tube babies). The external fertilisation of an egg before implantation in the uterus was first done for humans in 1978.
3) Drugs have been developed that stimulate the ovaries to release more than one egg. This has led to controversial sextuplet, septuplet or even octuplet pregnancies where few if any babies have survived.
4) Eggs, semen or even embryos can be frozen and stored for a long time before being allowed to develop into babies. This can be useful — e.g. healthy sperm might be stored before a treatment that could leave a patient infertile. However it means babies can be born when one or both of their biological parents are dead — raising concerns over who has the right to decide how the stored material is used.
5) The recent development of Viagra, a drug that treats male impotency (the inability to perform — not the same as infertility), has increased debate over what NHS funds should be used for.

Cloning and changing ethics

We agree. It is unethical to clone humans!

?

1) Human embryo research, the selective termination of embryos on the basis of genetic analysis (designer babies), cloning and even the genetic modification of humans are all now possible.
2) Dolly the sheep was cloned in July 1996.
3) Authorities have been set up to determine what is ethical medical practice — but they're finding it difficult to keep up with the issues raised by changing technologies.

Stop cloning around — there's some impotent stuff here...

Phew, some heavy stuff to finish up with, I'm afraid. This sort of thing crops up in the news a lot, so it's pretty hard to avoid some of it. You might not be able to avoid it in the Exams either, so it's as well to learn it. It's the kind of thing it's probably a good idea to know about anyway. As usual, when you think you know it, turn the page and scribble it all down. Then check you know it.

Summary for Enlightenment to Modern

At last, the end. Except for these questions, of course. So you haven't finished yet. In fact you haven't finished until you've passed those Exams — and until then you need to go over this stuff loads, until it's all sunk in. And don't forget — these questions are no substitute for practice on real Exams. So do attack a few past papers too — I know you'll love 'em.

1) Where did the technique of inoculation originate and by what route did it reach Britain?
2) Explain the difference between inoculation and vaccination.
3) What observation led Jenner to try vaccination?
4) Why was vaccination so important in America?
5) Discuss the influence of Government action on the success of vaccination.
6) Who opposed Jenner's discovery and why?
7) Would Florence Nightingale have been able to make the contribution she did without the effect of the Crimean War? Discuss.
8) What was the effect of the Franco-Prussian War of 1870 on the war against disease-causing micro-organisms?
9) Everyone needs a holiday. It worked for Chamberland. Explain.
10) Jenner and Pasteur both carried out experimental treatments on human subjects. Was either of them justified?
11) "Science isn't about individuals — it's about teamwork." Discuss this statement, with reference to the fight against germs. Mention at least three specific projects.
12) Write a short essay on the development of penicillin, covering the dates 1914 - 1945. Concentrate on illustrating the effects of the various "factors" outlined in section 1.
13) Why were dyes pursued so strenuously as a source for antibacterial drugs?
14) Why was the introduction of anaesthetics to surgery not welcomed by everyone?
15) Explain the negative effects of the introduction of anaesthetics.
16) Several factors delayed the widespread use of anaesthetics. Explain.
17) How does the work of Joseph Lister link surgery and public health — two themes that aren't often linked?
18) What is the difference between antisepsis and asepsis?
19) Why did blood transfusions not become common when they were first attempted in the 17th century?
20) How did science and technology in the form of the computer radically improve the potential of medical X-rays.
21) Christiaan Barnard — medical pioneer or self-important surgeon? Discuss.
22) Discuss the reasons why the advances in plastic surgery initiated by Archibald McIndoe occurred when they did.
23) Outline the shift away from "laissez-faire" by the British Government between 1831 and 1880, including the parts played by Chadwick and Snow.
24) Compare and contrast the attitudes towards public health in the Roman Empire with those of the British Empire in the nineteenth century.
25) What were the main innovations of the Liberal government reforms begun in 1906?
26) How did the London Blitz of 1940 help change attitudes towards the provision of publicly-funded health services?
27) Discuss the roles played by the two main architects of the Welfare State and the NHS.
28) "The last 25 years of the 20th century have seen a marked decline of trust in science and technology by the British public, especially in areas relating to health and medicine." Discuss.
29) What are the main health concerns of British people today? How do the threats of today's major diseases compare to those of past centuries?

Medicine Through Time Index

Medicine Through Time Index

Medicine through Time Index